RESPONSE TO

Have you ever been in a hurry when God wasn't? We live in a culture addicted to speed and ease. In his book God of the Long View, *David Wigington shares personal stories and scriptural principles of how God, in His love for us, works according to His timetable to accomplish His purposes. This is a great book, but take your time and enjoy the read.*

DOUG CLAY
General Superintendent of the Assemblies of God

"It takes time." Words we don't often like to hear. God, however, uses the oven as well as the microwave. David Wigington superbly illustrates how God is at work in our lives during the seasons when there are no quick answers. I highly recommend his book to you.

DR. GEORGE O. WOOD
Chairman, World Assemblies of God Fellowship

Standing in front of your microwave oven, tapping your foot because it is not working fast enough, may merely be an inconsequential inconvenience, but becoming frustrated or faithless when prayers seemingly go unanswered signals a need for a biblical understanding of God's nature. David Wigington's book, God of the Long View, *will reveal God's way and God's will. Read it and build your faith, restore your hope, and strengthen your trust.*

ALTON GARRISON
Assistant General Superintendent of the Assemblies of God

If everything is a miracle, nothing is a miracle. If God only does what we will when we will it, He is but our genie not our glorious Lord. David Wigington, in this excellent book, demonstrates why a long view of God is a high view of God. God, unbound by time, is ever at work according to His wisdom and greater purposes. God, who knows the end from the beginning, is indeed "unresting, unhasting...not wanting, nor wasting" and ever, lovingly at work.

DICK BROGDEN

Co-founder of Live Dead and Author of *Live Dead Joy*

Having traveled with David to many of the places described in this book, I have witnessed the God of the long view at work. David's thoughtful tracing of God's fingerprints and footprints through time should be a challenge and inspiration to all who do Kingdom work. I highly recommend this book to anyone who struggles when things in their life and ministry aren't accomplished as quickly as they had hoped.

ROD LOY

Lead Pastor, First Assembly of God, North Little Rock, Arkansas and Author of *3 Questions*, *Immediate Obedience*, *After the Honeymoon*, and *Help! I'm in Charge*.

I have long considered David Wigington to be one of the finest speakers I know. His written words are certainly the equal of his spoken ones. David's wit mixes well with his wisdom, and both prevalent in this charming volume! You will be blessed and entertained as you wend your way through these pages.

DAN BETZER

Lead Pastor, First Assembly of God, Fort Myers, Florida

For seventeen years of vocational ministry, I have been driven to leave my mark on eternity. God of the Long View has completely changed my perspective on the role I play in the Kingdom of Heaven. David's combination of storytelling and humor delivers a heart check that serves as a healthy reminder of God's great love for us and His plan to reconcile the world to Himself.

ADAM DETAMORE

Lead Pastor, Realife Church, Greenfield, Indiana

David Wigington's gift for memorable and inspirational story, when it comes to missions, is among the strongest I've encountered in my lifetime as a believer, a pastor, and a missionary. David's gifts are brought to this book and will help anyone wanting to motivate others about the Church's mission. Beyond knowing how to communicate, David is a great friend to missionaries all over the world and has helped in countless efforts to reach people beyond his own sphere. The investment you make in this book will make you richer when it comes to God's great cause!

ROBBY BRADFORD

Lead Pastor, River City Church, Lafayette, Indiana

For 20-plus years David Wigington and I have traversed the continent of Africa working together to see churches planted among the unreached. He is far more than a partner, he is a friend. David's passion for missions and missionaries has caused him to pour his life and resources into seeing people around the world encounter Christ. Along the way he has collected stories and has uncovered an amazing theme of how God works in history. As a missionary, this book is an encouragement and a testament to God's long view in establishing His Kingdom.

SCOTT HANSON
Missionary, Assemblies of God World Missions–Africa

David Wigington has written a book that deals with an immensely important subject in a remarkably accessible and engaging way. God of the Long View reminds us that God is both in control and active for our good, even when we cannot perceive it, and is almost certainly doing more than we could ever anticipate. In our fast-paced, demanding world, it is a necessary reminder for pastors and lay people alike. Wigington's style is light-hearted and yet direct. It would be hard to walk away from this book without being challenged to rethink our theology of God's rule in His world and in our lives. If you have someone in your life that struggles with the sovereignty of God, I highly recommend this book as a way of starting the dialogue.

JASON MCCLAFLIN
Director, Galilee Study Centre

David is a friend of mine and I can say this from watching his life up close, *he is one of the fastest people I have ever met! He talks fast, eats fast, moves fast, golfs fast, and yet he has the ability to see beyond fast into the long view and stay on course! If you struggle between fast and forever, this book is for you! You can be someone that wants to get it done right now and yet get it done the right way so that whatever you do lasts way beyond you and makes a difference for eternity!*

ROB KETTERLING

Lead Pastor, River Valley Church

GOD OF THE
LONG VIEW

*Trusting a Timeless God
in a Hurried World*

DAVID M. WIGINGTON

ISBN-13: 978-1-7330227-0-5

Printed in the United States of America.

The prayer by Cardinal Dearden featured in the opening and closing of this book was presented by Cardinal Dearden in 1979 and quoted by Pope Francis in 2015. See www.usccb.org/prayer-and-worship/prayers-and-devotions/prayers/prophets-of-a-future-notour-own.cfm (accessed January 29, 2019).

DEDICATION

To Shana, Nathan, Adam, Mom, and Dad,
and to my family at Cornerstone:

Thank you all for taking a "long view" with me.

TABLE OF CONTENTS

It helps, now and then, to step back and take a long view.

The Kingdom is not only beyond our efforts, it is even beyond our vision.

We accomplish in our lifetime only a tiny fraction of the magnificent enterprise that is God's work. Nothing we do is complete, which is a way of saying that the Kingdom always lies beyond us.

No statement says all that could be said.

No prayer fully expresses our faith.

No confession brings perfection.

No pastoral visit brings wholeness.

No program accomplishes the Church's mission.

No set of goals and objectives includes everything.

This is what we are about.

We plant the seeds that one day will grow.

We water seeds already planted, knowing that they hold future promise.

We lay foundations that will need further development.

We provide yeast that produces far beyond our capabilities.

We cannot do everything, and there is a sense of liberation in realizing that.

This enables us to do something, and to do it very well.

It may be incomplete, but it is a beginning, a step along the way, an opportunity for the Lord's grace to enter and do the rest.

We may never see the end results, but that is the difference between the master builder and the worker.

We are workers, not master builders; ministers, not messiahs.

We are prophets of a future not our own.

CARDINAL DEARDEN

INTRODUCTION

The other day on my way to make some hospital visits I tried an experiment. I got on the highway and drove exactly the speed limit—not under it, but right on the number (my truck has a digital display that shows the speed). I set my cruise control exactly on the speed limit—sixty miles per hour.

If you've never tried this experiment, I don't recommend it. Even though I was in the right lane, a guy in a U-Haul truck tailgated me, a bearded teenager in a Camaro flipped me off, and an old man in a Honda Accord yelled at me. One old lady went around me in her Taurus and turned and shook her head in disgust as she passed. In the 25-minute drive, people flashed their lights and honked their horns at me multiple times. They were all angry at me for slowing them down—even though they were the ones breaking the law. At least that's what I thought.

Because this was an experiment, I was keenly aware of everything happening around me and I was sure of one thing: I was driving exactly the speed limit. I looked in my rearview mirror to see the next reaction to my legal driving, and I saw lights. Yes, *those* lights. A state policeman was pulling me over, for what I assumed were congratulations on being a model citizen. He asked for my license and registration. He was gone several minutes before he returned and explained why he pulled me over.

"This is a really busy stretch of highway, Rev. Wigington. People are in a hurry to get to work and other places. I didn't actually clock your speed, but I noticed you were going significantly slower than everyone else, and in the state of Indiana it's against the law to impede the flow of traffic. I'm not going to write you a ticket today, but I need you to keep up with everyone else."

I was driving the speed limit, and I got pulled over because I was in less of a hurry than everyone else.

PRIME TIME

It seems like everyone is in a hurry. In fact, there are whole businesses built on that premise. I love Amazon Prime. Do you have it? If not, let me explain it quickly. You pay Amazon an annual fee, and in exchange you get 2-day expedited shipping on everything you buy on Amazon for the whole year. It's great. I can buy a book or a bookshelf or an electronic book reader or nearly anything else on Monday, and it arrives on Wednesday like clockwork.

Some readers remember a time before Amazon, eBay, and FedEx, while others can hardly imagine such dark ages! Some of you even remember a time before...wait for it...the Internet!

Let me sound old and wax nostalgic for just a minute. *When I was a kid*, if the local store didn't have something I wanted, I used our rotary phone to call an 800-number from a catalog and I placed an order for that item. Then I would wait. How long? That depends.

Maybe four or five days. Maybe four or five weeks. It gets worse. There was no Internet, and because there was no Internet, there were no tracking numbers. So once I ordered something, I waited and trusted that eventually it would arrive at my doorstep. I don't know if this ever happened to anyone else, but many times it took so long for my item to arrive that when it did come, it was like Christmas Day opening the box because I couldn't remember what I ordered.

But today, we don't have to wait. My town isn't one of them, but in some cities around the world, Amazon Prime gives buyers the option to pay a little extra for *same-day* delivery on nearly everything they buy. My wife doesn't even have to go into the store now to get her groceries. She places an order on the grocery store's app and on the way home from work swings into a designated front row parking spot. They bring her groceries out and load them into the back seat. We wait for almost nothing. Soon we won't have to stop by the store; we'll just trust a drone to drop it at our front door.

Have you noticed the "not-in-a-hurry" box when checking out on Amazon? There are usually three shipping options at various prices. The first and most expensive is for 1-day shipping. The second is for 2-day shipping (you get this for "free" with the paid annual Amazon Prime membership fee). Then there is a third box. The third option promises your item's arrival about a week later than the 2-day option. Next to the box it might say, "Not in a hurry? Choose FREE No-Rush Shipping." And sometimes they offer a monetary incentive like a dollar off a future purchase to use the "No-Rush Shipping." (I don't actually know how it works because I've never used it, and I bet you haven't either.)

When I order something, anything, I want it NOW! I'll often pay the extra $3.99 to get my item delivered the next day, but not because it's an emergency and I have to have it. I pay extra because I want it. That's the way I'm wired.

We have instant everything.

Why wait one week when you can have it tomorrow?

Why cook something all day in a crock-pot when you can microwave it? Why spend hours waiting for your chicken to cook on the stove when you can use your Instant Pot and have it ready in minutes? Don't have a microwave or an Instant Pot? Just order one on Amazon and tomorrow you will!

IN THIS BOOK

I won't speak for you, but my tendency is to always gravitate toward the quick solution. If something can cook it faster, deliver it faster, or fix it faster, then that's what I want.

This is one of the infinite number of ways that I believe God is different from us. God certainly *can* do anything He wants instantly! You'll read a story or two in this book about how God can do marvelous, miraculous, instantaneous things. More often than not, though, at least from our perspective, God checks the "not-in-a-hurry" box. More often than not, God chooses to work in ways that take time. Often, He works in ways that take so much time we assume He isn't working at all.

In this book, you will read stories of many times and places where God worked over time to heal, save, and build His Church. Some of these stories unfolded over a decade. Others took a lifetime. Still others spanned centuries.

What if God isn't in as big a hurry as we are? What if waiting is sometimes part of His plan? What if delay doesn't mean denial? What if God sometimes chooses to move in a time and in a way contrary to our nature?

If you are a pastor, I hope you find stories in this book that you can use to inspire your people to see God working and moving even if it's not what they expected. If you are a believer, I hope you find a balance to all the emphasis on the spectacular. I hope you find the stories of what God does over time to be no less spectacular and no less worthy of re-telling than stories of immediate healings or the dead raised. I hope you learn that even when God acts in the spectacular and the miraculous, He is very seldom spontaneous.
If you are a skeptic, I hope you find evidence in this book that God had you in mind centuries ago and still loves you very much.

CHAPTER 1

THE LONG RESTORATION BEGINS

*"You and this woman
will hate each other;
your descendants and hers
will always be enemies.
One of hers will strike you
on the head,
and you will strike him
on the heel."*

GEN. 3:15 (CEV)

I f you've been in the church for more than a minute or ever attended Sunday School, you've likely heard the story of creation.

It's a spectacular, supernatural, miraculous story! God created the world—the heavens and the earth—in six days, and then He rested.

Day One: God separated the light from darkness. Essentially in a day (or less) God created light.[1]

Day Two: God separated the waters above and below. Essentially in one day God created oceans and atmosphere.

Day Three: God created land and divided it from the waters he created in day two. Vegetation is created for the land.

Day Four: God created the sun, moon, and stars to fill the sky.

---

[1] This is pretty amazing to me. My mind can't comprehend light not separated from darkness or the other way around, but that's a thought for another time and place.

Day Five: God created all the creatures to fill the sky and water.[2]

Day Six: God created all the species of animals to populate the land. Adam and Eve are created as the pinnacle of God's created beings.

Day Seven: God rested.

That's an impressive week. Mankind has spent centuries and millennia trying to comprehend just little bits of what God created in such a short period of time.

For now, let's set aside whether or not this was a literal seven days or a figurative period of time (a discussion worth having another time). Any way you look at it, this was impressive work—supernatural work! I think a lot of people get caught up in the creation story and get stuck in arguments and ideas that completely miss the point.

God created the world.

He spoke it into existence.

And that's pretty amazing.

If you aren't careful, you'll miss the point of the creation narrative.

---

[2] Today, there are over 10,000 species of birds and over 31,000 species of fish and sea creatures.

THE FIRST GOOD NEWS

I attended the Broadway show *Hamilton* a couple years ago with my friend Rod and our wives. Rod is not much for theater. Everyone raved about how amazing *Hamilton* was. My friend was mostly bored out of his mind.

About halfway through, the cast began singing a song about the battle at Yorktown. The song built to a crescendo and at the end everyone on stage and everyone in the theater was clapping and yelling and celebrating. My friend heard the excitement and clocked in just long enough to ask, "What just happened?"

"We won the revolutionary war!" I explained with exclamation.

With the delayed reaction a turtle would be proud of, my friend leapt to his feet (after everyone else in the theater had calmed down) and yelled, "Yay, America! We won!" He caught the crescendo. He heard the celebration, but he missed the dialogue that gave it meaning.

If you aren't careful, you may read the first few chapters of Genesis the same way. You see all the pomp and circumstance and miss the dialogue that gives it meaning.

God created the world. BOOM!

Cue lights flashing and big musical number!

Adam and Eve walk in the Garden of Eden with God.

Cue the feel-good number with lots of great harmonies.

Adam and Eve sin. Snake. Apple. BOOM!

Cue lights dim, ominous music with minor chords and dissonant harmonies. Another big musical number.

We know all those stories. Even non-churchgoers can probably piece together the narrative. But what comes next is perhaps the most important part.

> You and this woman
> will hate each other;
> your descendants and hers
> will always be enemies.
> One of hers will strike you
> on the head,
> and you will strike him
> on the heel. (Gen. 3:15 CEV)

And there it is. Genesis 3:15 gives us the first glimpse of the plan of God. We see the first hint of God's long view plan to restore humanity to the kind of relationship with Him that Adam and Eve first enjoyed. This verse is what scholars call the *protoevangelium*. It comes from two words in the Greek—*protos* meaning "first" and *evangelion* meaning "good news" or later "gospel."

Speaking to the snake, God says, "You and this woman will hate each other; your descendants and hers will always be enemies. One of hers will strike you on the head, and you will strike him on the heel." That is the moment the long restoration begins. That is the moment God starts chasing us. That is the moment when God promises not to give up on us. That is the moment that God first promised to send us a Savior.

Early believers read this verse after the death and resurrection of Jesus and began to understand it for the first time as it was originally intended—as a prediction of the encounter Jesus would have with the snake at the cross. It was a prediction and a promise that God would not leave Adam and Eve or their descendants (us!) without hope. It was a promise that God would send someone to ultimately destroy the death they introduced to the world by their sin. But it was a promise that would take centuries to be fulfilled. Generations would live and die waiting for the fulfillment of the promise.

GOD KEEPS NO ONE WAITING

If God could speak the world into existence in six days, could the same God not also fix in a nanosecond what Adam and Eve broke in a moment? Could He not have just declared a fix for their sin right then and there?

I believe God can do anything, so...YES! God could have done that.

But marvel at this—He *chose* not to.

So why did He choose not to restore immediately? Why did God choose to restore through descendants rather than through Adam and Eve? Why did God choose the long view?

I think there are many reasons that God chooses the long view.

God values patience.

God values process.

God values perseverance.

God values perspective.

Remember, God's "long view" is only long from our perspective. God exists outside our time and knows the end from the beginning. We must reevaluate our "theology of time."

We will explore these reasons and more in the chapters to come, but for now the point I don't want you to miss is that Jesus was there from the very beginning. Jesus was not and is not some divine backup plan because the first plan didn't work. Jesus was *always* God's plan for restoring what Adam and Eve broke—and it would take centuries for Jesus to come. Thus, God's plan has always involved waiting. Jesus was not some bench warmer waiting to come into the game and score the winning points. He was not our rescuer in that sense.

Jesus did come to rescue *us* and to be a substitute for *our sins, but* Jesus has *always* been a part of God's long view plan for us. In other words, Jesus came to rescue *us*, not to rescue God's plan. From the very beginning onward, Jesus has always been the center and pinnacle of God's plan to restore humanity to Himself.

The prophet Isaiah talked about the new king with such anticipation and excitement that one might think the new king Jesus was waiting outside Isaiah's room for him to finish writing. But it was another 700 years before God's people could attach real meaning to the words "Wonderful Counselor, Mighty God, Eternal Father, Prince of Peace" (Isa. 9:6).

> *"Jesus was not and is not some divine backup plan because the first plan didn't work. Jesus was always God's plan for restoring what Adam and Eve broke."*

This is the salvation plan of God. You and I are a part of the story. We are a part of the drama unfolding to rescue humanity and restore creation to the Creator. The Germans call it the *heilsgeschichte*—the salvation history.

This is God's story. We betrayed Him, and ever since He has sought restoration. It's happening in beautiful ways and in unexpected places. It's happening on God's timeline and not ours. We know this for sure: God doesn't make us wait for no reason. He chose to make us wait so we could learn, grow, and become partners with Him in His pursuit of the lost.

C. S. Lewis said, "I am sure God keeps no one waiting unless He sees that it is good for him to wait."[3]

---

[3] C. S. Lewis, *Mere Christianity*, C. S. Lewis Pte. Ltd., 1980. XV.

— CHAPTER 2 —

A BRIEF THEOLOGY OF TIME

"Time flies like an arrow; fruit flies like a banana."

ANTHONY G. OETTINGER

I have a theory about time. I think time is more relative than we were taught as kids. We were taught that every day contains 24 hours; every hour, 60 minutes; and every minute, 60 seconds. A year has 365 days; a decade, ten years; and a century, ten decades. I remember tests on these facts in early elementary school. "Telling time" was one of the most rudimentary things we learned as children. Time is a constant. "Time marches on."

But what if we have it all wrong?

Stay with me here.

What if time, or at least our perception of time, is constantly changing?

Think of it this way. When you turned 5-years-old and just celebrated your fifth birthday, it seemed your next birthday was an eternity away. Rightfully so. At 5-years-old, one year is 20 percent of your life. Waiting until "next Christmas" or your "next birthday" for a certain gift was the seeming equivalent of a life sentence. It took forever for the calendar to turn from one year to the next.

I'm not knocking on the door of 50 years just yet, but I'm walking up the sidewalk with the door clearly before me. When I turn 50, the wait from my 50th birthday to my 51st will be the rough equivalent of two percent of my life. No wonder why the older I get, the more time seems to fly. Maybe every year seems to pass more quickly because with each passing year, 365 days is an ever-shorter period of time within the span of my whole life. (I didn't say my theory was scientific.)

Time is not actually moving faster ("flying"), but our perception of time certainly changes as we age. I can't tell you how often a past event comes to mind and my perception is it happened a "few" years ago. When I look up the occurrence, I discover it happened 13 or 14 years ago.

If our perception of time can change so drastically over the span of 50 years, it may be that we have been given a glimpse of why the Bible says that "a day is like a thousand years to the Lord, and a thousand years is like a day" (2 Pet. 3:8). Since we are temporal and God is eternal, this observation is just a fraction of the difference between our view of time and God's view. C. S. Lewis put it this way:

> If you picture Time as a straight line along which we have to travel, then you must picture God as the whole page on which the line is drawn. We come to the parts of the line one by one: we have to leave A behind before we get to B, and cannot reach C until we leave B behind. God, from above or outside or all

around, contains the whole line, and sees it all.[4]

GOD CREATED TIME

There was no clock before creation. There was no division between night and day. God created time.

For through him God created everything in the heavenly realms and on earth. He made the things we can see and the things we can't see—such as thrones, kingdoms, rulers, and authorities in the unseen world. Everything was created through him and for him. (Col. 1:16)

In the beginning the Word already existed. The Word was with God, and the Word was God. He existed in the beginning with God. God created everything through him, and nothing was created except through him. (John 1:1–3)

GOD TRANSCENDS TIME

When we see time as part of God's creation, we appreciate that He is not limited by it any more than He is limited by an aardvark or a wildebeest. He is "other than" His creation—all of it.

I am the Alpha and the Omega—the beginning and the end," says the Lord God. "I am the one who is, who always was, and who is still to come—the Almighty One. (Rev. 1:8)

---

[4] C. S. Lewis, *Mere Christianity*, C. S. Lewis Pte. Ltd., 1980. 168.

> Before the mountains were born, before you gave birth to the earth and the world, from beginning to end, you are God. (Psalm 90:2)

> Jesus Christ is the same yesterday, today, and forever. (Heb. 13:8)

This is not some deistic view that sees God as setting time in motion and then letting it go. He is not some great watchmaker who wound the clock of human history only to sit back and watch it wind down to destruction.

The transcendence of God in relationship to time does not mean He is indifferent to time, but it does mean that He knows the end from the beginning.

> You know what I am going to say even before I say it, Lord... You saw me before I was born. Every day of my life was recorded in your book. Every moment was laid out before a single day had passed (Psalm 139:4, 16).

Notice David did not shake his fist at God because God's foreknowledge somehow robbed him of his free will. Rather, David seemed to take comfort in knowing that God knew everything he would face the next day and the next day and the next. As should we.

Sov'reign Ruler of the skies,

ever gracious ever wise;

All my times are in thy hand, all events at thy command.

He that form'd me in the womb,

He shall guide me to the tomb:

All my times shall ever be, order'd by his wise decree.

Plagues and deaths around me fly;

Till he bids I cannot die;

Not a single shaft can hit, till the God of love sees fit.[5]

GOD INTERACTS WITH TIME

The Scriptures make it clear that this God who transcends time and space also interacts with His people in time and space. God's interaction in time and history is very clear, and His interaction with time and history was most clearly demonstrated in the life and person of Jesus. The incarnation (God becoming flesh) demonstrated that God transcends time but also makes Himself subject to time and operates within it to accomplish what He desires.

But when the right time came, God sent his Son, born of a woman, subject to the law. God sent him to buy freedom for us who were slaves to the law, so that he could adopt us as his very own children" (Gal. 4:4–5).

Jesus experienced everything just as we experience it—

---

[5] From the hymn "Sovereign Ruler of the Skies" by John Ryland.

including this frustrating limitation called time (see John 7:6).

Operating within time, Jesus came. He walked and talked with us, and then, at just the right time, died for us.

> For, there is one God and one Mediator who can reconcile God and humanity—the man Christ Jesus. He gave his life to purchase freedom for everyone. This is the message God gave to the world at just the right time (1 Tim. 2:5–6).

GOD HAS A PURPOSE FOR TIME

God doesn't just transcend and tolerate time. At the same time, God has a purpose for time. The ultimate plan for time—as God has drawn it on His divine paper—is to bring glory to Himself in the restoration of creation. Could God make another mark on His paper and instantly restore creation and bring glory to Himself? Sure, He could (remember, God can do anything). But He chooses to use time for His purposes, and since we exist in time and space, God's people are often the instruments He uses to accomplish His purposes:

> This truth gives them confidence that they have eternal life, which God—who does not lie—promised them before the world began. And now at just the right time he has revealed this message, which we announce to everyone. It is by the command of God our Savior that I have been entrusted with this work for him (Titus 1:2–3).

Time has meaning because of God's purposes. Time is not some cruel joke in which we wait for God's inevitable punchline. Instead, God invites us into the future He is creating with us. He allows us to be used in bringing glory to Himself and restoring creation to its Creator.

N. T. Wright put it this way:

> The point of the resurrection...is that the present bodily life is not valueless just because it will die... **What you do with your body in the present matters** because God has a great future in store for it... What you do in the present—by painting, preaching, singing, sewing, praying, teaching, building hospitals, digging wells, campaigning for justice, writing poems, caring for the needy, loving your neighbor as yourself—will last into God's future. These activities are not simply ways of making the present life a little less beastly, a little more bearable, until the day when

"Time has meaning because of God's purposes. Time is not some cruel joke in which we wait for God's inevitable punchline. Instead, God invites us into the future He is creating with us."

we leave it behind altogether... **They are part of what we may call building for God's kingdom.**[6] (emphasis mine)

The God of the long view sees time differently than we do. If we gain just a glimpse of His perspective on time, we might find more patience and understanding of how and why He acts. Sometimes God accomplishes in a day something that seems as though it should take 1,000 years. Sometimes God takes 1,000 years to accomplish things that we think should only take a day.

The God of the long view makes no distinction between those two because He transcends our time and space even as He uses us for His purposes within them. Many of the questions we ask God about time probably seem nonsensical to Him. C. S. Lewis mused about it this way,

> Can a mortal ask questions which God finds unanswerable? Quite easily, I should think. All nonsense questions are unanswerable. How many hours are in a mile? Is yellow square or round? Probably half the questions we ask—half our great theological and metaphysical problems—are like that.[7]

My brief theology of time concludes with this. God created time. God transcends time. He is not confined by time unless He

---

[6] N. T. Wright. *Surprised by Hope: Rethinking Heaven, the Resurrection, and the Mission of the Church.* New York City: HarperCollins Publishers Inc., 2008. 192–193.

[7] C. S. Lewis. *A Grief Observed.* New York City: HarperCollins, 1994. 80–81.

volunteers to be. Time doesn't control or limit God any more than a Lego ship controls or limits the child who puts it together. God is not oblivious to how long things are taking in your life. If we think God has lost track of time, it is we, not God, who need to reset our watches. God interacts with time and uses it for His purposes.

CHAPTER 3

HOW GOD WORKS

"I believe in the supernatural."

MYSELF

You might want to underline, circle, or highlight my quote to the left. I do believe that God can do anything. While God can do anything, the instantaneous, supernatural, miraculous intervention is not His normal course of action. He prefers (or at least He predominantly chooses) to work in other ways. As I look at Scripture, my own life, and the lives of those around me, my observation is that God's preferred method of working through His people is much more complicated than we have been led to believe. *Can* God do the instantaneous, miraculous thing? Yes! But more often, does He choose to take a long view of what He wants to accomplish in our lives? Also, YES!

I grew up in a Pentecostal/charismatic tradition that put tremendous value on the supernatural. I was a pastor's kid. I remember evangelists and missionaries coming through our church telling stories of the supernatural. I sat on the edge of my seat listening to a missionary from India tell a story about a young man healed of leprosy. I peeked out from underneath the pew I was playing under when the evangelist waved his handkerchief and talked about the cripple who couldn't walk until God touched him and now, he can walk. I believed every word. I still do.

I SAW IT WITH MY OWN EYES

I saw an actual supernatural, instantaneous, act-of-God, physical miracle one time. I was praying after a Sunday night service in my home church as a teenager. This was what one did on Sunday nights: go to church, worship, listen to announcements, listen to the preaching (usually a special guest speaker), go to the altar and pray for a bit, then head to Noble Romans or Chi Chi's for a late Sunday night dinner. This particular Sunday night was different. I remember it like it was last night. Every movement played out before me like a slow-motion drama.

The guest musician/preacher said he felt "impressed" (in our tradition, this is a way of saying God is speaking to someone) that he should pray for the sick and that God might want to heal someone. This was not new. From the time I was a very young child, I remember my dad (the pastor) and others praying for anyone who was sick and believing God for healing. I saw this "healing prayer line" perhaps a thousand times, and there was always someone who declared he or she had been healed. Up until this night, I never saw a healing I could "verify" with my own eyes. I'm sure I witnessed someone being healed in those prayers, but I couldn't see it. I believe God can deliver someone from pain, migraines, or whatever, but I can't always see it.

But this night was different. From the corner of my eye I watched a husband roll his wife down the aisle in her wheelchair. I knew them. I knew her. This wasn't some made-for-TV-evangelist moment.

These were my friends. She had multiple sclerosis (MS) and had been confined to that wheelchair for a couple years. They were a faithful couple. We saw them every Sunday. As they approached the front of the healing prayer line, I grew nervous. I don't know why, but I was nervous. I thought, "What if God doesn't heal her? That would be disappointing. But what if God does heal her? Wouldn't that be amazing? But what if He doesn't?"

She reached the front of the line. My pastor and the guest evangelist greeted her. They laid their hands on her and prayed. I stretched out my hand and prayed for her from the altar step I sat on about 20 feet away. The prayers reached a fever pitch and then died down. This is how these things usually went—we prayed and not much happened. But this time as the prayers died down, something different began to happen. I watched as the guest evangelist reached out his hands and motioned for the woman to stand up.

Panic set in. The knots in my stomach did an aerial show worthy of Cirque du Soleil.

"What does he think he is doing?"

"Doesn't he understand she really can't walk?"

"He's going to hurt her."

"This is embarrassing."

And then it happened. She stood up. Holding tightly to the evangelist's hands, she was a little wobbly at first, but like a sailor getting her sea legs, she stood upright. She stood there for what seemed like an eternity.

Then she began to walk.

I saw it with my own eyes. Someone I knew who couldn't walk was walking, and that moment made a lasting impression on me. It's one of the reasons that to this day I believe God can do anything He chooses.

God got a tremendous amount of glory for Himself that night. To be sure, the glory was spread around a bit, too. The evangelist got some. The pastor got some. I got some because I was "in the room." Maybe, after all, it was my prayer from 20 feet away that put the healing "over the top," so to speak. But God got most of the glory.

A JOURNEY OF A MILLION STEPS

After four and a half decades of life and over two decades as a lead pastor in full-time ministry, that is still the only verifiable miracle I have ever witnessed. I believe that God can do anything. And yet, only one time in my life have I actually seen a verifiable, instantaneous, miraculous physical event.

I still believe. I still pray for the sick. I still encourage others to believe and do the same. But my observation is that often God chooses to bring glory to Himself in ways other than the instantaneous, supernatural physical miracle. He's the God of the long view. It helps to remember that. It helps to remember that even when you can't *verify* it, God is working to bring glory to Himself through His creation. God does many miracles. He can do incredible things instantaneously. I've seen Him heal someone physically. I've seen Him change hearts—both my own and other people's. I've seen Him deliver people from addiction. I've seen Him save sinners.

Fast forward about a decade from that story of healing. I left home and went to college and seminary to prepare for ministry. I came to Bloomington, Indiana with my wife and our 6-month-old son to plant a church in 1997. Our new church, Cornerstone, met for the very first time on March 9, 1997. Ron and Mary were among the few dozens in attendance for our first service. Mary was in a wheelchair. When I introduced myself to them, Ron explained Mary's condition: "She has MS."

"God chooses to bring glory to Himself in ways other than the instantaneous, supernatural physical miracle. He's the God of the long view. It helps to remember that."

My brain moves pretty quickly to conclusions. It's a blessing and a curse. In that moment, my brain immediately connected Mary and her condition with the healing I had seen a decade ago. I thought (thankfully, I didn't verbalize), "This is amazing. God can heal MS. I've seen Him do it. God will heal Mary and that healing will propel our church and my ministry, and wonderful things will happen because God's got this. He can heal MS."

Only this time, He didn't.

We prayed—at church, at the hospital, at Mary's home. We believed. We prayed. We pleaded. For almost a decade we prayed. And then Mary died.

Does that mean that God loved her less? Does that mean that God didn't want to bring incredible glory to Himself? Of course not. God did use Mary's life for His glory. It just wasn't instantaneous. God still brought great glory to Himself in Mary's sickness and even in her death. Doctors, nurses, co-workers, and friends saw Mary patiently endure her weaknesses while she leaned into Christ's strength. They saw her suffer without complaint and give God glory for even the smallest of victories. God patiently used the life of a woman with MS to point people to His glory every moment of every day including her very last. When I visited Mary in her home right before she passed, she gave me instructions for her memorial service. She looked at me and said, "Pastor, you have to help people understand that I didn't lose this battle. Jesus already won this battle against MS before I was ever diagnosed. You have to tell them that when I was weak, He was strong."

What I now believe and hope to show you here is the beautiful ways God is working over incredible lengths of time with a long view to bring glory to Himself and build His Church. Much like He did through Mary's life. This is a book about a way, not often highlighted or even acknowledged, that God chooses to work.

The supernatural, miraculous, instantaneous work of God is a beautiful thing, and it still happens. But when it does, God is not changing the order of the world in which we live. Our world is still broken. The supernatural is more like a high-five from God. It's like God breaking into our present time and space and showing us what eternity with Him will be like. It's the exception, not the rule.

Miracles, by definition, are not *normal*; they are exceptional. Yet, somehow our theology devolved to demand that the exceptional be normal. Because we now demand or expect that God will constantly act in ways not normative for Him, we experience disappointment and disillusionment with Him. We need to "reset" our view of God in this sense. We need a new spiritual lens prescription so we can see that He constantly works on our behalf over time to bring glory to Himself and accomplish His work in us.

Walk the aisles of a local Christian bookstore or search the religious books category of Amazon. A lot of books have been written about the supernatural, including near-death and post-death experiences. A lot of people have shared their encounters with the miraculous. This book is about a different way that God works—a less flamboyant way, a less marketable way, a way with a smaller television audience. This different way in which God works is consistent, reliable, and just as biblical as the supernatural, miraculous acts. What follows are accounts from friends around the world who are seeing God move and bring glory to Himself in significant ways. Sometimes His work took years and even decades, sometimes centuries (not that my friends have been around for centuries).

If a supernatural miracle is a high-five from God, this view of God over time is a long embrace, it's a journey of a thousand, or even a million, steps. Going forward, I trust you will find a reminder that everything God does is worth waiting for and that even when you don't see or feel Him, He is faithfully at work accomplishing His ultimate plan to restore all of His creation to Himself.

CHAPTER 4

GOD AND THE GOLDFISH

"There is no reason to regret that I cannot finish the church. I will grow old, but others will come after me. What must always be conserved is the spirit of the work, but its life has to depend on the generations it is handed down to and with whom it lives and is incarnated."

ANTONI GAUDI

M any regard La Sagrada Familia, a cathedral in Barcelona, Spain, to be among the most beautiful buildings in the world. And they regard it as such even though it remains unfinished. The cornerstone of the basilica was laid in 1882 and construction moved forward under the direction of architect Antoni Gaudi in 1883 and continued until his death in 1926. It is still under construction today. A celebration of completion is planned for the centennial recognition of the architect's death in 2026. If completed by then, the building will have been under construction for 144 years.

Even though people's appetite for the immediate was nothing like today, people of Gaudi's day grew impatient with the long process of construction. Gaudi did not. When people asked him when the basilica would be completed or even if it would be completed in his lifetime, Gaudi was fond of saying, "My client is not in a hurry."

And it's true. God, Gaudi's client, was not, and is not, in a hurry.

THE EIGHT-SECOND ATTENTION SPAN

But we are. In 21st-century Western culture, our appetite for the immediate is insatiable. We have instant everything. We have never been in a bigger hurry. And we love it.

A Microsoft report published in 2015 reported that the average attention span fell from 12 seconds in the year 2000 to eight seconds in 2015.[8] According to the report, an 8-second attention span is less than the attention span of the average goldfish. (Side note: This means if you have read this far, you are exceptional or a freak of nature. I'll let you decide which one.)

We have so much available at the touch of a button, and it's a button we don't even have to push anymore. We have Wi-Fi-controlled light bulbs in our home. We can walk into the living room and say, "Alexa, turn on the lights," or "Alexa, turn off the fan," and just like that, it happens. I've grown so accustomed to this that some days I walk into my office which is not equipped with this technology and get irritated when I actually have to flip the switch to turn on my lights. (Moment of honesty: There are days when I work in the dark for a couple of hours because I forgot to flip the switch when I walked in. Pathetic, I know.)

We don't have to wonder about anything. What year was this movie produced? What year did that song reach number one? How old is

---

[8] "Microsoft Attention Spans Research Report." Spring 2015. https://www.scribd.com/document/265348695/Microsoft-Attention-Spans-Research-Report

that actor or actress? There is no more wondering or typing into Google or turning the pages of an encyclopedia (if you remember those). Just ask Siri or Alexa or Google.

None of these is inherently wrong or evil, but they have changed us. Technology has measurably reduced our attention spans. Satya Nadella, CEO of Microsoft, says, "We are moving from a world where computing power was scarce to a place where it now is almost limitless, and where the true scarce commodity is increasingly human attention."[9] Herbert Simon, Nobel Prize winner in Economics in 1979, says that all this information has changed us and consumed us. "[What information consumes is] the attention of its recipients. Hence a wealth of information creates a poverty of attention."[10]

While there is no Microsoft study to back up this claim, I think the reduction of our attention span has also resulted in a species-wide reduction in our ability to have patience.

We lack patience with one another. (I've been talking to Jesus a lot lately about my road rage.) Marriage is becoming more and more "old school" in Western culture. We lose patience so quickly with one mate, we'd rather not be married as marriage is a legal obstacle to quickly moving on to the next relationship.

---

[9] Ibid.
[10] Ibid.

We lack patience with our jobs. I know one person who has had seven jobs in the last 18 months. Oddly enough, there is always something wrong with the *job*, not the person.

We lack patience with our stuff. I have more than one friend who traded cars because they had no patience to get new tires or brakes. Crazy, right? But it's true. We are more apt to throw things out and start over than to find out what's wrong and fix it.

We lack patience with God. Our propensity to witness the supernatural and our proclivity to receive immediate answers cause us to think that either God is not at work or that God has forgotten us altogether.

We lack patience with ourselves. Change takes time. The kind of change God wants to make in us is more difficult than simply changing our diet or exercise routine. God wants to institute *real* change in our lives. He wants to change our nature, modify our desires, and alter our thought life. That kind of change takes patience and time.

Some in my generation will scoff at these inclinations and blame them on the tendencies of generations other than ours. But these are not millennial problems or even American problems—they are human problems.

We lack patience. When the God of the long view works patiently behind the scenes to restore us to Himself, we tend to miss it because our eight seconds is up. Like the goldfish who circles the bowl and forgets what she just saw, we forget the myriad of ways that God has patiently worked on us and in us.

So is God wholly incompatible with 21st-century Western culture? Have we lost hope because we can't pay attention long enough to see what God is doing? I don't think so. And I hope not.

When you only have an 8-second attention span, you tend to speed up and get all you can in that eight seconds. You also only tend to care about what happens in that eight seconds. We race from experience to experience. From high to high. No desire to slow down and remember or reflect. Like an Indy car racing around a track, we have no other aim but to go hard and to go fast. But if we are to find God, if we are to see how He is working and weaving His plan into the fabric of who we are, we will have to slow down and remember.

"...if we are to find God, if we are to see how He is working and weaving His plan into the fabric of who we are, we will have to slow down and remember."

Despite recent reports from Microsoft, I don't think humanity has changed all that much since millennia gone by. We've always had a hard time remembering. We've always had a tendency to not remember God's intervention and not see Him working in our lives. I think that's why God's people were always building memorials. In Joshua 4, God led His people safely across the Jordan and He then instructed Joshua to lead the people in building a memorial, so they would remember.

> Joshua chose twelve men; he called them together and told them: Go to the middle of the riverbed where the sacred chest is, and pick up a large rock. Carry it on your shoulder to our camp. There are twelve of you, so there will be one rock for each tribe. Someday your children will ask, "Why are these rocks here?" Then you can tell them how the water stopped flowing when the chest was being carried across the river. These rocks will always remind our people of what happened here today. The men followed the instructions that the Lord had given Joshua. They picked up twelve rocks, one for each tribe, and carried them to the camp, where they put them down. Joshua had some other men set up a monument next to the place where the priests were standing. This monument was also made of twelve large rocks, and it is still there in the middle of the river. (Josh. 4:4–9 CEV)

While the Israelites didn't have Alexa, it's possible their attention span wasn't much better than ours (perhaps better than eight seconds, but still miniscule in light of God's eternal perspective). Maybe we all should set up memorials to help us remember what God has done.

Remembering is a key to developing patience and perspective. Remembering what God *has done* opens our eyes to see what He is *doing*. In other words, remembering connects directly to patience. We lack patience with ourselves, others, and God because we never stop to remember what has been accomplished in the past.

To illustrate I'll offer a childhood memory. I used to hate going out to eat, especially to really nice restaurants. I loved the food, but I hated the time it took to get it. For a child, the time between the ordering of food and the delivering of food seemed like an eternity. Over time though, I began to connect the wait for the food to the food itself. I began to understand that a Big Mac was faster than filet mignon, but it wasn't better. I began to associate the wait of a nice restaurant with the quality of food that would eventually come my way.

We need that perspective on waiting outside the realm of food. We need to associate the waiting times in our lives with the fact that the God of the long view is working to accomplish something *better*. There's a bastardized gospel offered in parts of Western Christianity today. It populates many books and TV shows that deceptively promise *faster*. Jesus promises *better*. Don't settle for a Big Mac when you can have filet mignon. What God has in store is worth the wait.

When you remember the things He has done, you can appreciate what He is doing and the time it is taking. Remember the greatest gift God ever gave humanity was His Son, Jesus, and Jesus came after a period of waiting that lasted centuries.

Rather than thinking, "the longer I wait, the more God has forgotten me," we need to think, "the longer I wait, the more beautifully and powerfully God must be working on my behalf. He must be cooking up something wonderful."

Gaudi, the architect, was right—God is not in a hurry.

But we are.

We need less hurry and more wait. Dallas Willard fondly said, "Ruthlessly eliminate hurry from your life." C. S. Lewis said it no less eloquently in *Mere Christianity*:

> It comes the very moment you wake up each morning. All your wishes and hopes for the day rush at you like wild animals. And the first job each morning consists simply in shoving them all back; in listening to that other voice, taking that other point of view, letting that other larger, stronger, quieter life come flowing in. And so on, all day. Standing back from all your natural fussings and frettings; coming in out of the wind.[11]

---

[11] C. S. Lewis, *Mere Christianity*, C. S. Lewis Pte. Ltd., 1980. 198.

I've observed it in my own life and even seen it in the lives of my children. When we do things in a hurry, they are seldom done with excellence. The God of the long view works slowly, patiently, and diligently, restoring humanity to Himself and building His Church. But if we don't slow down, look, and maybe build a memorial or two, we will just circle the fishbowl and miss it. That's one reason I chose to memorialize many of the stories in this book. Because I need to remember what God has done in me.

CONNECTING THE DOTS

Ever wonder why companies pay for advertising on race cars? A car racing past at 220 miles per hour is just a blur. At some point though, the car slows down and pulls into the pits, or even better, pulls into victory-lane, and people notice the ads. It's kind of ironic. Pennzoil doesn't pay for the advertising it gets when race cars actually race; it pays for the advertising of its brand when the car stops. High definition television and 4K resolution in broadcasting have distorted this even more. Cameras track race cars going 200-plus miles per hour, but on our television screens we see clearly what cannot possibly be seen in person. Wrecks are viewed in slow motion. A brilliant pass in turn three is slowed down and "tele-strated" in great detail. Then if you're like me watching something previously recorded, you fast forward through the commercials or skip them altogether.

Maybe that's what we need—a spiritual camera lens through which to see things. Wouldn't it be wonderful to slow down the times that God really moves in order to really relish them? Wouldn't it be great to fast forward through the difficult times? Instead, we find ourselves speeding up what we should slow down and slowing down what we should speed up. Perspective is learning to slow the right things down. We need to somehow slow the throttle of our fast-paced existences enough so that what God is doing becomes less of a blur. We need to slow down enough to see what He has written in His Word and on our hearts. God has an eternal attention span. He is focused on eternal matters. Our attention span is eight seconds—literally. Our spiritual attention spans are just as short. We need to slow down and let our eight seconds intersect with eternity.

Do you remember "Connect the Dots"? In case you were deprived as a child, I'll fill you in. "Connect the Dots" was a page with a series of numbered dots. You find dot 1 and draw a line to connect dot 1 to dot 2, and so on and so on. Elementary coloring pages might only have 20 dots to connect. More advanced pages might have hundreds. Before the dots are connected, they make little sense, they look random, messy, and nonsensical. But once you connect all the dots and step back, an image you "draw" by simply connecting the dots is revealed.

There are times connecting the dots makes little sense because the dots to be connected are not right next to each other. Perhaps to connect dot 16 to dot 17, you have to search the page to find dot 17 on the opposite side and draw a line that covers most of the page. And sometimes while examining any segment of a "Connect

CONNECT THE DOTS

•16

•17 •15

•19 •13

•18 •14

•24 •23 •9
•22 •10 •8

•21 •20 •12 •11
•28 •29 •4 •5

•25 •27
•26 •6 •7

•30 •3

•31 •2

•33 •32 •1 •49
•48
•34

•47
•35 •37 •44
•36 •45 •46

•39 •38 •43 •42

•40 •41

the Dots" page, you see a jagged, incomplete line. That line never makes sense until the picture is complete, and you hold it up and see the whole picture.

Any given eight seconds in life is one of those little, jagged, nonsensical lines between the numbers 42 and 43. We have to learn to trust the One who put the dots on the page. What looks random here may be a part of His beautiful design. What looks messy in our 8-second observation may be something beautiful He planned out. In eternity we will see all the dots connected, and hopefully, by the time you finish this book, you will see the potential of beautiful things emerging from your dots.

God is eternal. We are temporal. Much of our frustration with the God of the long view comes from this tension. We are afraid of "running out of time." This is not a concern of God's. Our temporal existence flows from and connects to His eternal existence. He broke into our temporal existence with this eternal existence in a moment we call the incarnation—when God became human. God is not disconnected from our time and place, nor is He limited by it. He sees more than we see and knows more than we could ever know. We need to patiently wait and understand that the God who made the fishbowl wants to show us the universe outside our eight seconds. He wants to teach us to breathe eternal air. He wants us to see the world and more specifically, our circumstance, from His eternal perspective.

CHAPTER 5

THE LONG-VIEW POSTER CHILD

"There is no indication that God explained to Joseph what He was doing through those many years of heartache or how the pieces would eventually fit together. He had no ways of knowing that he would eventually enjoy a triumphal reunion with his family. He was expected, as you and I are, to live out his life one day at a time in something less than complete understanding. What pleased God was Joseph's faithfulness when nothing made sense."

JAMES DOBSON

Knowing the end of a story can have a significant impact on how we view the middle of it. The movie *The Sixth Sense* was great—the first time. Once you know the ending, you never watch the movie the same way ever again.[12] This is why I don't watch Hallmark movies. They all have the same storyline. Every. Single. Time. Knowing the guy will get the girl at the end, and everyone will live happily ever after sucks the life from every Hallmark movie for me. Could they not mix things up just a little bit *at least one time?*

The first time I heard the story of Joseph from the Bible, I was on the edge of my seat in a Sunday school in Crawfordsville, Indiana. We didn't read the story all at once, and since I couldn't read yet, I had to wait from one Sunday to the next to hear what happened. (That's an anticipation I love trying to recapture whenever I read Scripture.)

If there is a poster child for the idea of the God of the long view, it has to be Joseph. You have probably read or heard Joseph's story

---

[12] Spoiler: Bruce Willis' character is dead the whole time.

many times, but try to forget it for a minute or two. This might be a challenge, but it's one we should endeavor to tackle whenever we read a narrative portion of Scripture. Pretend you don't know the ending and walk through this story with me.

THE JOURNEY OF A TATTLETALE

Joseph was 17-years-old when his story begins in Genesis 37. He was the son of Jacob and he worked for his stepbrothers. He was also a tattletale. (I can relate. When I was a kid, I loved to tattle on my big sister.) Joseph was born when Jacob was very old, which made Joseph really special to his dad. Joseph was a daddy's boy, and daddy gave Joseph gifts that he didn't give to the other kids. (What happened next might be kind of predictable, like those Hallmark movies.) The prized gift that Jacob made for Joseph was a multicolored coat. The reaction of Joseph's brothers was natural—they hated him. They had nothing nice to say about Joseph.

Joseph then had a couple of elaborate dreams about his brothers and himself. In the dreams, it was clear to Joseph that one day his brothers would all bow down to him. Youth and insecurity got the best of him, and Joseph's situation with his brothers went from bad to worse. Joseph ranted to his brothers and told them about the dreams. He certainly was not a model of wisdom at this young age. (Pro tip: If you have a dream you believe is from God that involves you ruling over your siblings or them bowing down to you, don't share it. Hold onto it.) The jealousy and hatred of the brothers toward Joseph grew by the minute, and I don't blame them. Joseph had the lack of wisdom you might expect from a 17-year-old boy, and it cost him big time relationally.

Joseph's dad asked him to go and check on his brothers who were pasturing the sheep. This is another strike against Joseph—he's the only son not working. As Joseph drew close to where his brothers were keeping the sheep, they saw him coming, and all their jealousy and anger escalated into a murderous plot. They plotted to kill Joseph and throw him in a hole and tell their dad that a wild animal ate him.

Reuben, the firstborn and one of the more level-headed brothers, proposed a compromise. Reuben surmised they wouldn't actually have to kill him. Instead, they could just throw him in the hole. Joseph wouldn't be able to climb out without help and eventually he would die. The brothers liked this plan. They waited for Joseph to arrive, took his multicolored coat, and threw him into the hole.

Now Reuben planned to return later and rescue Joseph, but during lunch the brothers saw a caravan of traders passing by. The brothers concluded it was wasteful to let Joseph just rot away and die when they could sell him to this traveling band of merchants and slave traders. He would be carried off to a foreign land and be someone else's problem, and they would be a little richer. The brothers (minus Reuben) agreed and sold Joseph for 20 pieces of silver to the traders who then took him south into Egypt. This was fraternal dysfunction at its worst. Joseph certainly had not been a model brother, but he didn't deserve this, did he?

Remember that Joseph didn't know the end of the story. Can you imagine the hurt he experienced being treated by his own brothers like that? This teenager was now alone and probably afraid on a journey that led him hundreds of miles from home. If you dropped into that cistern or walked next to Joseph, hands tied together in a string of other slaves walking through the desert, you would have likely witnessed a dejected, discouraged young man. If you looked at Joseph in that moment and said, "Hey, Joseph, isn't it amazing how God is working in your life," he might have laughed at you—or worse.

Reuben returned in an attempt to rescue Joseph from the hole and, of course, Joseph was gone. His remaining brothers concocted a scheme to cover their betrayal. They took Joseph's coat, covered it in goat's blood, and sent it to their dad. He concluded that a wild animal ate Joseph.

Meanwhile, back on the trail, Joseph was sold again, this time to Potiphar, an officer of Pharaoh, the king of Egypt. Potiphar was a powerful man—definitely not the kind of man you wanted to mess with—and Joseph worked hard for him. He succeeded again and again in this foreigner's home. Potiphar was so pleased with Joseph, his work, and his success that he made Joseph his personal attendant. He put Joseph in charge of everything. Joseph was doing great, and Potiphar and his house were doing great. But...Joseph was still a slave. He was just a young man, and we can imagine that he missed home, his dad, and maybe even his brothers. Eventually, Potiphar put Joseph in charge of everything that he owned.

The Genesis narrative comments at this point that "the Lord was with Joseph" (39:2). I wonder if Joseph knew that at this moment. Betrayed by his brothers, sold not once, but twice. Now in charge of everything. Even then, Joseph was a servant in a foreign land. Could he possibly know the Lord was with him? His circumstances may not have led him to believe that.

Then, just as it seemed that Joseph hit his stride, things became difficult again. Joseph had a run-in with Potiphar's wife. She tried to seduce him multiple times. Joseph refused again and again until one day Potiphar's wife grew so mad, she grabbed his cloak as he ran away. She used the cloak to concoct a lie about what happened. Potiphar's wife lied about the encounter and told her husband that Joseph made the advances and she refused him. Understandably, Potiphar was irate and threw Joseph in prison.

Joseph seemed more mature by this point in the story. He wanted to do the right thing. Potiphar's wife pursued him, and he declined. Now Joseph, betrayed by his brothers, sold not once, but twice, landed in prison. And by prison, I mean dungeon. This is not a prison like we know today—no cable television, no workout room, and no visitors from home. Joseph's situation went from bad to worse. But we read another comment at this point of the story in Genesis. Interjected in the narrative, as if to remind us the story isn't over yet, the Bible says, "But the Lord was with Joseph in the prison" (v. 21). The Lord was with him? This doesn't mesh with our "bless me" theology well. In a day of microwave Christianity, when we pray for something in the morning and God has not intervened by noon, we assume He has abandoned us. The concept that God could be *with* Joseph in prison runs a bit counterculture.

Deliver Joseph from prison? Yes!

Miraculously transport him to a tropical island? Sure!

Make gourmet food appear before him? You bet!

But be *with* him in prison? That doesn't neatly fit into our way of thinking about God.

Nevertheless, Joseph once again rose to the top in prison. Pharaoh's cup-bearer and baker were thrown into prison with him. They each had dreams and Joseph interpreted them. The dreams and interpretations had totally different outcomes—the cup-bearer was to be restored and the baker was to die. Both of these came true just as Joseph said. Two more years passed. Joseph was still in prison. God was apparently still with him, but could Joseph see it at this point?

Then Pharaoh had some dreams and no one was able to understand or interpret them. It was then the cup-bearer remembered the foreigner in prison who interpreted dreams. Pharaoh called for Joseph and with God's help he interpreted Pharaoh's dreams. Pharaoh's dreams predicted seven years of good times and great crops, followed by seven difficult years of famine. Joseph suggested

Pharaoh gather food during the good years and store it up so there would be enough when the bad years came.

Isn't that fascinating? Joseph had a God-given gift to interpret dreams. When he was young and immature, he used that gift to build himself up. But when he was more "seasoned," he used the same gift in God-ordained ways to benefit others. (There are unhealthy ways to utilize your divine gifts. Use your giftedness wisely with God's big picture in mind.)

Pharaoh said to Joseph,

> "I hereby put you in charge of the entire land of Egypt." Then Pharaoh removed his signet ring from his hand and placed it on Joseph's finger. He dressed him in fine linen clothing and hung a gold chain around his neck. Then he had Joseph ride in the chariot reserved for his second-in-command. And wherever Joseph went, the command was shouted, "Kneel down!" So Pharaoh put Joseph in charge of all Egypt. And Pharaoh said to him, "I am Pharaoh, but no one will lift a hand or foot in the entire land of Egypt without your approval." (41:41–44)

As I read the story, I nearly shout out loud: "Now the Lord is with Joseph!" But the truth is, whether Joseph saw or felt it, the Lord was with him the whole time. Joseph's circumstances went from bad to worse to more worse to a little better to way worse, and now he was one of the most powerful people on the planet. Here's the thing: Joseph's circumstances changed while God had not. The minute you give your circumstances the power to alter your view of God, you no longer really believe in the omnipotent Yahweh God of the Bible.

> *"The minute you give your circumstances the power to alter your view of God, you no longer really believe in the omnipotent Yahweh God of the Bible."*

Things happened the way Joseph interpreted, and Joseph led Egypt in preparation for the famine. When the famine came, it seemed Joseph and Egypt were the only ones prepared. Joseph's dad sent his brothers (all but his youngest brother Benjamin) to Egypt to buy grain. Joseph recognized them, but they didn't recognize him. He used a series of tests to mess with them. (Don't judge. You might do the same. I would.) Joseph gave them grain, kept one brother, and sent the others back making them promise to bring Benjamin to him. Joseph messed with them some more. (Come on, they sold him; he could have a little fun, yeah?) After a while, Joseph could wait no longer to reveal his identity.

"I am Joseph!" he said to his brothers. "Is my father still alive?" But his brothers were speechless! They were stunned to realize that Joseph was standing there in front of them. "Please, come closer," he said to them. So they came closer. And he said again, "I am Joseph, your brother, whom you sold into slavery in Egypt. But don't be upset, and don't be angry with yourselves for selling me to this place. **It was God who sent me here ahead of you to preserve your lives.** This famine that has ravaged the land for two years will last five more years, and there will be neither plowing nor harvesting. **God has sent me ahead of you** to keep you and your families alive and to preserve many survivors. **So it was God who sent me here, not you!** And he is the one who made me an adviser to Pharaoh—the manager of his entire palace and the governor of all Egypt. Now hurry back to my father and tell him, 'This is what your son Joseph says: **God has made me master over all the land of Egypt.** So come down to me immediately! You can live in the region of Goshen, where you can be near me with all your children and grandchildren, your flocks and herds, and everything you own. I will take care of you there, for there are still five years of famine ahead of us. Otherwise you, your household, and all your animals will starve.'" Then Joseph added, "Look! You can see for yourselves, and so can my brother Benjamin, that I really am Joseph! Go tell my father of my honored position here in Egypt. Describe for him everything you have seen, and then bring my father here quickly." Weeping with joy, he embraced Benjamin, and Benjamin did the same. Then Joseph kissed each of his brothers and wept over them, and after that they began talking freely with him (45:3–15 emphasis mine).

When they finally realized who Joseph was, the brothers were dumbfounded. They must have wondered if this was the moment their necks would feel the cold steel of Joseph's sword. Was this payback time? Rather than payback, Joseph offered reassurance. Four times he told them it wasn't their misdeeds that sent him there, but God.

> **Verse 5:** "It was God who sent me here ahead of you to preserve your lives."
> **Verse 7:** "God has sent me ahead of you to keep you and your families alive and to preserve many survivors."
> **Verse 8:** "It was God who sent me here, not you!"
> **Verse 9:** "God has made me master over all the land of Egypt."

It is in this moment that we begin to see the God of the long view at work. God was planning all along to spare Joseph's family. God's hand directed all the confusion, all the brokenness, and all the jealousy toward His ultimate gracious goal.

THE BIG PICTURE OF A TATTLETALE

One interesting thing to me about Joseph's story is that the *whole* story seems to be about the *bad* actions of men and women. Brothers sold him into slavery. Potiphar's wife falsely accused him. Potiphar imprisoned him, falsely accused. But at this moment in the story we realize that this isn't about the *bad* actions of men and women at all. It's about the *good* actions of a loving God. This is the theme of Joseph's story: God was with him. Robert Longacre calls this the "macrostructure" of Joseph's story: "Joseph's brothers, meaning to harm him, sold him into Egypt, but in reality, God sent him there so that he could save Jacob's family and many others from death by starvation."[13] Each scene in the story, Longacre argues, relates to the macrostructure.

Joseph lived in exile from his family from age 17 until his reunion with them at roughly age 40. For 23 years, things mostly didn't go the way Joseph might have expected or wanted, but at every turn God positioned him to be at the right place at the right time to not only essentially save humanity, but to also reunite with his family. After two decades, Joseph reiterated his understanding of the macrostructure of what God accomplished in his life:

> But Joseph replied, "Don't be afraid of me. Am I God, that I can punish you? You intended to harm me, but **God intended it all for good**. He brought me to this position so I could save the lives of many people. No, don't be afraid. I will continue to take care of you and your children." So he reassured them by speaking kindly to them. (Gen. 50:19–21, emphasis mine)

---

[13] Robert Longacre. *Joseph: A Story of Divine Providence: A Text Theoretical and Textlinguistic Analysis of Genesis 37 and 39-48*. University Park, PA: Eisenbrauns, 2003. 43.

The dream, cistern, slavery, second slavery, false accusation, prison time, dreams, interpretation of dreams, and command over Egypt, they all related to the macrostructure of Joseph's story and life. We can see that, and with the benefit of time and perspective, even Joseph saw it at the end. I sincerely doubt he saw the connection between his slavery and the macrostructure of God's plan while it happened. God had a long view in place for the role Joseph needed to play in His redemption story—a macrostructure.

> *"Only when you begin to take the long view will you have the ability to connect the painful dots of every circumstance to the beautiful thing God is doing."*

What if your story has a macrostructure as well? What if every episode of your life— the good decisions and the bad, the high moments and the low—are all part of God's macrostructure? Only when you begin to take the long view will you have the ability to connect the painful dots of every circumstance to the beautiful thing God is doing.

I love this view of life with God. I love it because it means God can use even my immaturity, my mistakes, and my misuse of His given gifts to me. It also means I can stop blaming other people for all the bad things that happen to me. It's liberating as I begin to see the terrible things that other people do as pieces of the giant puzzle God is putting together so I will be at the right place at the right time to fulfill my destiny.

What if Joseph isn't the only poster child of the long view? What if every one of our lives has a macrostructure that God works together for our good and for His glory? If that's true (and I think it is), then we should look at every moment of our lives through that lens. Perhaps we need some "Joseph goggles." Through these goggles we could see that when people betray us, it's part of God's plan and He hasn't forgotten us. When falsely accused, the goggles would remind us that what we need in that moment is not justice, but God's plan (which involves global and eternal justice). Wearing these goggles, we remember that when we rise to the top, it's not for our own benefit, but for the benefit of others and for the glory of God. When we crash to the bottom, the goggles remind us that God can (and will) bring glory to Himself in the cisterns and prisons of life. We remember that God sees the whole story arc even while we only live a moment of it and that God might be preparing us for something in this moment that we cannot possibly anticipate or see decades later in our story.

As a pastor, I encounter a lot of people who reduce their story to what other people did to them. It would have been easy for Joseph to do the same. But what if your story is like Joseph's? What if your story isn't about the bad actions of other people at all? What if your story is also about the good that God is doing that won't be seen until the great *reveal*?

CHAPTER 6

THE ONE-ARMED PREACHER

"And we know that God causes everything to work together for the good of those who love God and are called according to his purpose for them."

ROMANS 8:28

I love a deal. I love to save money.

Best Buy, one of my favorite stores, used to send coupons to my house. The coupon said I could save 10 percent off *my entire purchase*. That was great news! I could use a new MacBook Pro or a new iPad or a new camera lens (and in case you're feeling generous, I could still use all those things). The coupon always had a problem: an asterisk. The asterisk sent you looking for additional information in the fine print at the bottom. Inevitably, the asterisk led to "some exclusions apply." And "some exclusions apply" typically meant the coupon covered *nothing* I actually wanted to own.

> **"Understanding the God of the long view requires perspective, and perspective requires time— sometimes loads of it."**

That's the way many people view verses like Romans 8:28: "God causes everything to work together for the good of those who love God" (*some exclusions apply). The thing is, there is no asterisk. Paul says that "God causes everything to work together for the good of those who love God and are called according to his purpose for them." PERIOD. No asterisk. No long list of exclusions. But if we only apply our 8-second attention span, we never see the truth in that. Understanding the God of the long view requires perspective, and perspective requires time—sometimes loads of it. I learned this at a pretty early age.

MY DAD HAS ONLY ONE ARM

The story of how my dad came to have only one arm is...amazing. The day after Christmas 1964, my dad went to work. My dad worked in the meat department of a small locally owned grocery store in West Terre Haute, Indiana. Most of the products in the meat case were ground daily, and the equipment used was most certainly below today's standards and maybe even the standards of the mid-1960s. The meat grinder itself was in a dimly lit corner of the department. The machine, designed to be at eye-level, sat low, resting on top of a rigid plastic milk crate. The safety guard that covered the grinder's opening was deemed an inconvenient impediment to quick and efficient grinding and had been removed somewhere in the machine's history.

The process for grinding hamburger was much the same as today. The first time through the grinder, the meat emerges looking like spaghetti. Another pass or two through the grinder and it looks like everyone's idea of ground beef. Occasionally, a bone made its way into the grinder, and when it hit the augers, it made a terrible crunching sound.

On this morning, fresh from the delight of Christmas presents and meals, David Lee Wigington (or as I affectionately call him, "The Real David Wigington") ground some beef and proceeded to clean the machine so he could make ham salad. To properly clean the machine, several pieces had to be removed, cleaned, and reattached to the grinder, but as in any profession, there were shortcuts. My dad was taught that to prep the machine for grinding a new product, the fastest way to clean the places you couldn't reach with a rag was to turn the grinder on and let it vibrate all the loose pieces out the opposite end. He and others in the department had performed this procedure hundreds, if not thousands, of times without incident. But that day there would be an incident—a life-altering, potentially life-ending incident.

As my dad leaned over to reach the power switch with his left hand, he was holding a cleaning rag in his right hand. As his torso dipped to reach the switch on the back side of the machine, the rag in his right hand apparently slipped into the opening normally protected by a safety guard. The rag was just long enough to reach the churning augers. The augers grabbed the rag and before he could let go, his right arm was sucked into the meat grinder. From that moment on, his life would never be the same.

The blur of what happened next is exactly what you might imagine. The crunching of bones in the meat grinder was not unusual, but the realization that they were *his* bones was frightening. This was not just the sound of a stray bone the butcher missed in a slab of ground beef. This was the awful sound of 45 bones from finger tips to elbow being crushed and mangled.

He let out a scream that alerted everyone in the store as to what happened, and they leapt into action, sort of. Communication was drastically different in 1964. They called the telephone operator and instructed her to make four phone calls—to the store owner, a local doctor, the ambulance service, and the hospital to alert them of an incoming trauma.

The store owner arrived almost immediately.

The local doctor never arrived.

The hospital eagerly anticipated the incoming trauma.

But the ambulance was nowhere in sight.

In the chaos and confusion, they called for the ambulance service from the wrong side of town. Ambulance services were independent contractors often run by funeral homes (how was this ever a good idea?). If you needed an ambulance, you called for the one nearest you to be dispatched. That didn't happen that day. The operator called for an ambulance from Terre Haute, and the grocery store was in West Terre Haute. For those unaware of rural Indiana geography, these are two separate towns separated by several miles and a river. For what seemed like an eternity, the ambulance didn't come. The delay was long enough that a mechanic across the street noticed the commotion and came to grocery store with his tools offering to reverse the motor on the grinder and pull out the remains of the arm. Dad decided if anyone should work on him, it should be a doctor and not a mechanic, so he politely declined.

Approximately 25 minutes after the initial calls went out, the ambulance finally arrived. The ambulance attendant walked into the meat department and assessed the situation. "Who put a tourniquet on his arm?" No one had. The only first aid of any kind administered was a wet rag to his forehead (which he held with his left hand and hadn't even been wrung out). After the attendant learned that no one put a tourniquet on his arm, he asked the question that revealed to my dad that perhaps there was some sort of divine, miraculous intervention: "Well then, where's the blood?" In 25 minutes of waiting, with the flesh of his forearm shredded like ground beef, my dad had not bled one drop of blood. They loaded him up with the grinder still attached to his arm and took him to the hospital where surgeons completed the amputation the grinder started.

While it was clear that God was with my dad that day, he still woke up the next morning as a 16-year-old without a right arm. There was no guardian angel to swoop down and swat the rag away before it got stuck in the grinder. There was no miraculous healing and rejoining of bone and flesh. Just a 16-year-old kid with no right arm.

If the story stopped there, it would be fair to wonder if Romans 8:28 was really true. Does losing one's arm ever really work out for "good"? Can something so gruesome and tragic be used by God for a 16-year-old's good and for God's glory?

GOD WASN'T DONE

Fast forward 15 years. My dad was around 30 and I was 7 or 8. I had listened to my dad, the "one-armed preacher," recount the story that you just read in gruesome and fascinating detail my whole life. (Also, the phrase "busier than a one-armed paper hanger" holds true. I've seen the reality of it, and it's pretty funny.) I heard my dad tell his story and give glory to God so often and so consistently that I disconnected it from the reality of what truly happened. One evening I crawled up on my dad's lap and declared, "Dad, I hope I lose my right arm in a meat grinder when I'm 16." He had to explain to me that it wasn't quite as glamorous as it sounded.

It sounds silly to think that an 8-year-old would hope to lose his arm, but it reveals something very powerful about perspective. I wasn't there. I didn't feel the pain. I didn't wake up as a 16-year-old without an arm. I didn't have to learn how to tie my shoes with one hand or put on socks or wear a hook prosthesis. But time and distance from the event gave me something that 16-year-old in the hospital couldn't possibly have had—perspective. From my proverbial seat on the bus, I saw how God turned something tragic into something good for my dad, and I certainly saw how God was beginning to get the glory for this terrible accident.

But God wasn't done.

A lot of families have Christmas savings accounts or vacation funds. It's not uncommon for families to save money for Christmas or a week at Lake Tahoe. My family was different. We had an ongoing savings account for the next arm my dad would need. He wore a hook prosthesis which required replacement every few years. Insurance didn't cover it because it was considered "cosmetic." But one year, dad got a giant hug from God in the person of the late David Wilkerson (author, pastor, and founder of Teen Challenge). Wilkerson was in town to speak at a meeting my dad was in charge of, and he asked dad why he didn't have a one of those "new-fangled bionic arms I saw on TV." (This is not an actual quote, but it's the way I like to imagine him saying it.) Dad explained he received no settlement for his accident and the new "bionic" arms were very expensive. Wilkerson took out a piece of paper and wrote "IOU $10,000" on it. He handed the paper to my dad and said, "If it's more than that, let me know. I want to buy you one of those arms."

Dad was soon fitted with a "bionic" (or more accurately, myoelectric) prosthesis, and my dad, the one-armed preacher, became the bionic man. Dad got a little more "good" worked from an awful situation, and God got a little more glory. That arm lasted much longer than it should have, and by the time it needed to be replaced, the price had risen substantially—to $25,000. This time dad's hug from God came in the form of a four pastor friends who raised the money and bought him a new arm. Dad got a little more good, and God got a little more glory.

Every year for Christmas my dad got a new glove and a new battery. The cosmetic glove that covered the prosthesis always became dirty and needed an annual replacement. The battery wasn't lithium ion like today's batteries, so it lost capacity throughout the year and needed replacing. But this second prosthesis began to age, and there was no path to a new arm. Mom and dad decided to go order a new arm and finance it.

One afternoon in 2006, dad walked into the prosthetics company in downtown Indianapolis where a man named Don Hedges worked. Don had known my dad since shortly after his accident and had taken care of his prosthetics since he was 16. Don shouted from across the room: "Dave, I'm glad you came in this week and not next week, because I'm retiring and I would have missed you." He shared the news that workers' compensation laws in Indiana had changed. The state changed the coverage classification for prosthetics from cosmetic to mandatory for patients who never received a significant financial settlement. That day, dad got another hug from God, but this time in the form of a man who made and fitted fake arms for a living and who was retiring in a few days. If dad went to order his new arm the following week, it's possible we may have never learned about the new law. It took someone like Don Hedges who had known dad's case for over 40 years to understand that this new law might apply to him. If he could prove that his original claim was a workman's comp claim, then all prosthetics would be covered from this point forward. But could he *prove* it?

He called his mother who lived in the same West Terre Haute house where he was raised. She could have been a star on HGTV's "Hoarders" if the show aired a decade earlier. Stacked floor to ceiling, file boxes of bills, newspapers, and whatever else hoarders hoard filled every room and hallway in her house. It took several days and lots of digging, but finally my octogenarian grandmother found one paystub. It was one of the 52 checks my dad received every week for a year after his accident. The check was for the amount of $28.11. The total compensation he received for losing his right arm was $1,461.72. The paystub proved his original claim was a workers' comp claim. His injury was grandfathered in and covered moving forward. Dad got a new arm, this time paid for by workers' compensation. A few years later he got another new arm. This time the arm was equipped with a new "Michelangelo" technology and had a price tag north of $75,000! This new technology allowed my dad to do something I never saw him do before—he was now able to cut his own steak! Dad got a little more good, and God got a little more glory.

A few years later, dad began having problems with his left shoulder. Only one "good" arm made any problem, injury, or surgery on that arm monumentally challenging. The surgeon said dad required rotator cuff surgery. The surgery was scheduled to take a couple of hours. We knew there was a problem when the surgeon entered the waiting room only 15 minutes after dad was wheeled back to the operating room. There was a big problem. The surgeon calculated that because dad was overusing his one "good" arm since he was 16, his left shoulder now showed the signs of wear and tear that one would expect in a person over 100 years old. There was nothing left of his rotator cuff and nothing the surgeon could do but close him up and tell us that dad would never be able to lift anything above his shoulder again. But dad worked hard in therapy. He learned to use different muscle groups, and over the next several months he regained a strength the surgeon said he would never have again. Dad got a little more good, and God got a little more glory.

In 2012, I got an urgent call from my mom. She and my dad were in Florida for a conference and dad was helping set up. They were hanging a banner, and as he lifted his side of the banner, his left shoulder dislocated. Again, with only one good arm, any injury is catastrophic. The shoulder was put back into place at the ER, but we learned over the next few weeks that the damage was already done. When the shoulder dislocated, it caused significant nerve damage. Dad lost total use of his "good" arm. I've never seen my dad so low. He never accepted his deficiencies as a handicap. He always just worked twice as hard as everyone with two arms to make up for the fact that he only had one. But now he was dejected. Defeated. It was hard to imagine any good coming from this.

But then it got worse. Since the dislocation, doctors said the nerves might eventually regenerate, but that would take time. Several months after the injury, dad had the nerves tested and the report was devastating. The nerves were dead. There was no coming back from this. My dad would have to live out his days without the use of either arm. He could still use his left hand but couldn't lift it away from his body. He had one good hand and one good shoulder. Unfortunately, they weren't on the same arm.

I've never heard my dad despondent, but now he was. He never talked about regretting things he couldn't do or mentioned his physical limitations. But this was different. My dad had golfed one-handed for several years. He was bad—I mean, really bad at golf—but we both got great enjoyment from our time on the course and from the great shots he occasionally hit. The day the news arrived about the nerves in his left shoulder, all he thought about was that he promised my son Nathan that one day he would take him golfing. Now that promise would have to be broken. "Pa" and Nathan would never have

> *"God offers us a promise. He promises that our story can work out for our good and His glory. No asterisk. No exclusions. No exceptions."*

their golf outing. Dad sobbed. I stayed strong until the moment the phone called ended—and then I lost it. How could this possibly be God's plan?

This time the hug from God came in the form of a person who heard my dad preach. This person was a nurse who had worked in a  specialized field of nerve therapy and regeneration. At the end of the service, he came forward and told dad about a new therapy being done that showed promise in the regeneration of damaged nerves. When you're desperate, you'll try anything. Dad signed up for the therapy. Slowly, the nerves in his left shoulder showed signs of life. And I'm not talking about some immeasurable "feeling" that it was improving. I'm talking about nerves that once tested so low doctors said they were dead and gone were now registering life. Almost six months to the day after dad began the regenerative nerve therapy, he stepped up to the first tee at Wolf Run Golf Course in Zionsville, Indiana, with his oldest grandson Nathan. A promise was kept. Pa and Nathan got their golf outing. Dad got a little more good, and God got a little more glory.

Take any eight second slice of my dad's story, and it's unlikely you'll see how God was causing it to work for his good. But my dad is a living, breathing example of God's presence over time. God has been at work in his life. God's work in my dad's life has not really been the spontaneous, instantaneous kind. It's more like the kind that is decades in the making. This kind of work reveals itself with time, patience, and perspective. My family has seen it. Dad's grandkids have had a front row seat to the mystery and majesty of a God who works in the long view to see that everything works together for good for His kids. God offers us a promise. He promises that our story can work out for our good and His glory. No asterisk. No exclusions. No exceptions.

CHAPTER 7

PATIENCE OF A JANITOR

"Before you marry a person, you should first make them use a computer with slow internet service to see who they really are."

WILL FERRELL

T he kind of patience required to slow down and see what God is doing certainly doesn't come naturally and it's not easy to acquire.

The God of the long view requires us to have a long view as well; it's just that we don't do well with the long view in our "have it now" society. We all want a mansion, but we don't want to work for it. We want it now! This kind of mentality birthed and now sustains the lottery. We know statistically it's more likely to be struck by lightning while drowning than to win the lottery, but we buy tickets anyway. Why? Because the lottery is a tax for the statistically challenged? No. Because the lottery holds the promise that we can have what we want without waiting or working for it.

Patience is a big key to seeing what God is doing.

> Dear friends, don't forget that for the Lord one day is the same as a thousand years, and a thousand years is the same as one day. The Lord isn't slow about keeping his promises, as some people think he is. In fact, God is patient, because he wants everyone to turn from sin and no one to be lost. (2 Peter 3:8–9 CEV)

Christians love to quote this verse, that to God "a thousand years is the same as one day." The problem is, we only seem to interpret and hold onto one side of that equation. We love the idea that a supernatural God can do in one day what might otherwise take a thousand years. But we don't often grab the other side of that principle—that sometimes God may take a thousand years to accomplish something that we think should only take one day.

> **"When we think God is acting slowly, He's actually being patient."**

The God of the long view doesn't have a Timex or a Rolex. He doesn't carry His iCal on His iPhone or His Google calendar on His Android device. Peter makes it very clear: When we think God is acting slowly, He's actually being patient.

EXAMPLES OF PATIENCE

We need a patience with God that mirrors His patience with us. God is working—if we can only slow down and trust Him. We need the patience of a janitor. Yes, I know that's not the saying. The saying is, "the patience of Job" or "the patience of a saint," but I like my version better. We'll get to that janitor in a minute, but first take a look at what James says about patience.

My friends, be patient until the Lord returns. Think of **farmers** who wait patiently for the spring and summer rains to make their valuable crops grow. Be patient like those farmers and don't give up. The Lord will soon be here! Don't grumble about each other or you will be judged, and the judge is right outside the door. My friends, follow the example of the **prophets** who spoke for the Lord. They were patient, even when they had to suffer. In fact, we praise the ones who endured the most. You remember how patient **Job** was and how the Lord finally helped him. The Lord did this because he is so merciful and kind. (James 5:7–11 CEV, emphasis mine)

This is one of my favorite New Testament passages because James spells the point out clearly. Five times in five verses James uses a form of the word patience. It's clear then that this passage is about... wait for it...patience.

James uses three specific examples of patience so we can learn the principles of patience. James tells us to learn from the farmer. What do we learn from the farmer? How much control does the farmer have over the rain and the sun? He can't make it rain. He can't make the sun shine. So what does the farmer do? He waits. He waits for the land, sun, and rain. He honors the process.

God is a wise husbandman, who "waiteth for the precious fruit of the earth, and hath long patience for it" (James 5:7). **He cannot gather the fruit until it is ripe.** He knows when we are spiritually ready to receive the blessing to our profit and His glory. Waiting in the sunshine of His love is what will ripen the soul for His blessing. Waiting under the cloud of trial, that breaks in showers of blessing, is as necessary. **Be assured that if God waits longer than you could wish, it is only to make the blessing doubly precious.** God waited four thousand years, until the fullness of time, before He sent His Son. Our times are in His hands. He will avenge His elect speedily. He will make haste for our help and not delay one hour too long.[14] (emphasis added)

From the farmer, *we learn that we have to be patient even when things are beyond our control.*

James then tells us to follow the example set by the prophets. This may be the lesson about patience we like least. Our culture, and even our Western church, often tell us we deserve to be happy, we deserve to have things go our way. While the "pursuit of happiness" is in the Declaration of Independence, I'm having trouble finding it in my Bible for some reason.

The prophets were a picture of happiness, weren't they? Daniel was in the lion's den. Jeremiah was thrown into a cistern one minute and into prison the next. Elijah was alone by the Cherith Brook (his

---

[14] Andrew Murray. *Waiting on God.* Scotts Valley, CA: CreateSpace Independent Publishing Platform, 2017. 60–61.

obedience to God got him sent to a place literally called "Cut Off"). These were obedient prophets doing exactly the right things and they were treated with injustice. Life wasn't fair! They delivered God's message to the people and still awful things happened to them. Why did bad things happen to good prophets?

Many people become disillusioned with God after encountering false teachings about prosperity and happiness that are popular in the church today. Husbands and wives sit in my office and justify divorce because, they say, "God wants me to be happy." Parents justify allowing their young children to abandon church because sitting in church "doesn't make them happy." We've been sold on a lie. God never promised we would feel good. God never promised we would be happy. He promised suffering (John 15:20). He promised us persecution (Matt. 10:16ff). He also promised joy on the other side of that suffering. (Later, we'll talk about the difference between the American pursuit of happiness and the promise of joy.) Now, in case this is still unclear, James makes it explicit:

> My friends, be glad, even if you have a lot of trouble. You know that you learn to endure by having your faith tested. But you must learn to endure everything, so that you will be completely mature and not lacking in anything (James 1:2–4 CEV).

Many people become disillusioned with God after encountering false teachings about prosperity and happiness that are popular in the church today.

Nobody wants to write a book about that, though some possible titles could include:

21 Ways to Suffer for Jesus in the Next 21 Days

Six Easy Steps to Great Persecution

How to Walk with God and Die Young

I can see that last title just flying off the shelves. The pursuit of happiness was a dream of the American forefathers, but your heavenly Father has something better in mind for you. He wants to restore you to Himself, and that process requires the patience of the prophets. From the prophet's example, *we learn to be patient even when we are treated unfairly or unjustly*. When things don't go your way or when things don't go as quickly as you hoped, don't assume God left you.

> **"The pursuit of happiness was a dream of the American forefathers, but your heavenly Father has something better in mind for you."**

The last example about patience that James gives us is Job. Job was another person who did right, and his circumstances turned out all wrong. Job learned to trust God and have patience even when he didn't understand. James says that "the Lord finally helped him." Job never received answers, but he received help.

In our information age, in which we're overloaded with information and access to answers, I wonder if we will make the same exchange with God. Will we, like Job, trade our demand for understanding to just have a God who is with us? It's not an "unalienable Right" as the pursuit of happiness is written in the Declaration of Independence, but we certainly feel like we have a "right to know." The lesson we learn from Job is simple but powerful: *We learn patience with God when we give up the right to know and take the opportunity to hold His hand.* Persevere because God's plan is at work even when we can't see it or understand it. Job didn't know what was happening, but he knew God. We need to learn to let that be enough for us.

AND NOW ABOUT THAT JANITOR

In Istanbul, there is a place called the Grand Bazaar. It's fascinating and massive. It dates back to the days when travelling caravans of merchants sold their goods along trade routes. They arrived in town and set up shop for a day or two before moving on. Towns then built structures to house the merchants, their camels, and their wares to keep them safe from the elements and from thieves. These covered stalls enticed the merchants to stay for longer periods of time, and over time they became permanent structures.

Today, the Grand Bazaar has 61 covered streets and over 4,000 shops. Nearly a half million people visit every day. On a cold day in December, I was one of the half million. The shop stalls lining either side of the street are approximately 15 feet apart, and in the street between the shops, thousands of locals and tourists walk shoulder to shoulder looking for spices, silk, trinkets, or gold.

Gold is a big deal in this part of the world. It's a measure of wealth. Banks aren't necessarily trusted in the same way they are in the West, so many keep their life-savings in gold. Gold is also a measure of love. It's said, the more gold a woman wears to a wedding, the more her husband loves her. Several of the 61 covered streets are dedicated to gold merchants. There's an amazingly warm quality to the light on these streets, even on a cold day. Everywhere you look is the reflection of deep, rich, yellow gold.

In the middle of this scene, a man—the janitor—saw an opportunity. He noticed something as he swept the streets of the Grand Bazaar. In the dust, dirt, and cigarette butt-filled waste, he occasionally saw something glistening. It was gold. Not much of it, but it was gold. And so began his long view approach to life and retirement. He swept the streets of the Grand Bazaar every day, and every night he searched the trash to find the gold. He collected particles of gold dust that had floated through the air from jewelers' shops and off the hands of customers who handled jewelry. He found miniscule pieces of broken gold that flaked off of an ornately carved bracelet. He found tiny sections of gold chain that fell to the floor, forgotten after a jeweler shortened a necklace to the prescribed length. Little by little, his stash of gold grew—one particle at a time. By itself each particle was barely, if even, measurable, but still he continued accumulating. At first, he only had a few grams, but eventually he had a few kilograms until he amassed a fortune in gold. As he approached retirement, people started to notice something. The janitor wore different clothes and shopped in places janitors never shopped. One day he found a nice house, some would say a mansion, and everything was paid for by gold dust collected over a lifetime of labor one particle at a time.[15]

We need to learn the patience that the apostle James teaches—the patience of a farmer, the patience of a prophet, the patience of Job—and even, dare I say, the patience of a janitor. Sometimes it seems that God is absent from our world when the opposite is actually true. He's there, and His beauty is visible if you look close enough. God's beauty is most evident in the least likely places—in the gutters, the broken places, the trashed places, the forgotten places. His presence glimmers with great beauty, but it takes great patience to see it. God is working with patience to restore humanity to relationship with Him. He is building communities of faith in difficult places—one speck of beauty at a time.

---

[15] That story sound unbelievable? Apparently, there's a lot of valuable stuff in our streets. A street-sweeping firm in England recently announced plans to "mine" the things it swept off the streets in the United Kingdom. Veolia Environmental Services says that every year nearly $1.25 million dollars of precious metals are swept up on the streets of the U.K.

CHAPTER 8

THE LOST GOLFER

*"Isn't it funny how day by day nothing changes,
but when you look back everything is different."*

C. S. LEWIS

Jesus saves! (That's another line you might highlight and remember because what I'm about to say runs counter to much of what is taught in evangelical circles.) And God can do anything, remember? I believe Jesus can save people instantly! This is the church worldview in which I grew up and which I still believe today.

"Is there sin in your heart?"

"Raise your hand!"

"I see that hand!"[16]

"Pray this prayer and you can be saved!"

Just like that...viola! A sinner becomes a saint.

---

[16] Admit it! You were like me, looking around when your head was supposed to be bowed, and more often than not, when the preacher said he saw a hand, there really wasn't one, or at least you didn't see one.

It's not wrong. Jesus can radically, supernaturally, spontaneously change someone's life. He does! I believe it! But I grew up with the impression that this was the only way God saved people. As it turns out, it's not. God often takes a long view, even of our salvation.

About 15 years ago, a missionary friend told me it could take up to seven years for a Somali Muslim to become a follower of Jesus Christ. When I heard that, something inside became almost judgmental of my missionary friend. I thought, "If it takes you seven years for someone to become a Christian, then you're doing it wrong. I can accomplish that in 30 seconds at the end of my sermon on Sunday."

A PROCESS OFTEN PRECEDES THE MOMENT

Then I met Craig. Craig was a PGA Tour player. I met him at the driving range in 2001. We struck up conversations about life and golf and became fast friends. Craig and I went to lunch. I met his wife. He met my wife and kids. At first, he called me "Preacher," which shortened to "Preach" over time. Craig is the reason nearly no one knows my actual name now. God willing, I will have grandkids in a few years, and I am even now actively campaigning to keep them from calling me "Preach" as they grow up.

I wanted to get to know Craig, but honestly, in the back of my mind, I was keeping score. I knew that God was no "respecter of persons," but I sure was. Notching a PGA Tour player on my "people I got saved" belt would be great for me as a pastor (no, I don't actually have a belt; it's an LED scoreboard in my office). Seriously though, in the world of pastor wins and losses, I believed that would be a good win, and I thought, "If I could only get him to church, then he'd get saved!"

Easter came. Craig and his wife came to church, and I preached my heart out. I believed this was the moment. We gave everyone a response card that Easter and asked them to check a box indicating where they were on their journey with Christ.

- I'm a committed follower of Jesus Christ.
- I'm on the journey, but I'm not there yet.
- Today I'm making a decision to follow Christ.
- I'm not interested.

After service, I rushed to retrieve the response forms. I flipped through them until I found his name. There it was: "I'm not interested." I was devastated. I followed the playbook and did everything I was supposed to do. I did my part, and now Jesus was supposed to do His. This was supposed to be the moment.

But it seemed that moment would never come. The next Easter came and went. "I'm not interested." Another Easter came and went. "I'm not interested."

Through the years, Craig had two little girls who affectionately called me "Uncle Preach" (or "Uncle Peach" when they struggled with their r's). I was a lot of things to Craig—caddy, marriage counselor, friend, even designated driver at times. And every year when Easter rolled around, he dutifully came to church, endured an hour of singing and preaching, and filled out his card: "I'm not interested." One year, he even went out of his way to explain to me that he meant no offense by his response, but that he came on Easter to support me, not because he was interested in following Jesus.

Hard times came. An ugly divorce. Then Easter. Only that year, the answer was a little different. Rather than the "I'm not interested" box, Craig filled out a response card with a checkmark next to the box which said: "I'm on the journey, but I'm not there yet." It took another whole year. The next Easter, Craig, now a single dad, came to service with his two little girls in tow. This year he couldn't wait to fill out the response form. I had prayed for this moment for the better part of a decade. I still have the response card in my office with his name and a checkmark next to the box that read: "Today I'm making a decision to follow Jesus."

Does Jesus save? You better believe He does. Is that salvific moment often culminated in a "decision" or a "sinner's prayer"? Of course, it is. But more often than not, years of process precede the moment. I believe the God of the long view values that process. I actually think He treasures the process. God was pursuing Craig from the moment he was born, and even before. What was another few years to God? It was an eternity for me, but for God it was just a second or two (remember that day being like a thousand years, etc.). If you popped in for an 8-second view of what was happening in Craig's life, you might not have seen the process happening. From day to day, it probably didn't look like much of anything changed. He and I often reminisce. More than six years after his baptism, he's married to a great woman who loves Jesus. Looking back now, everything has changed.

Before I met Craig, I think I placed too much value on the moment (or the decision) and not enough value on the process. This mentality became pervasive in our church—it adversely affected our views of church growth and the mission field. We get excited when a handful of people in a full stadium of thousands who have heard the gospel a hundred times decide to "rededicate" their lives to Jesus or a few raise their hands and "get saved." We should get excited! It's beautiful. The angels in heaven rejoice, and so should we. God is restoring people to Himself. But we should be just as excited about the missionary worker in Somaliland that is four years into that 7-year relationship that will culminate in a young Somali lady risking her life to follow Jesus. We should be just as excited about the worker in a CrossFit gym in the Middle East who works all day in the gym for a 60-second window to share the gospel with his Muslim friend at the end of a team workout.

INVESTING IN THE PROCESS

One could say that our retirement accounts have ruined our view of missions and outreach to the lost. We view everything in terms of return on investment. If I invest $500 every month in my retirement account, I expect to see a certain return on my investment. Now, if I can get a better return with another fund, another firm, or another type of account, then that's the one I want. I want the highest return on investment for my dollar.

Sadly, this mentality has infiltrated our view of missions. We love seeing a measurable return on our investment in missions. So much so that I've even heard pastors (perhaps inadvertently) attach a dollar value to a soul: "For every $3 you give, someone somewhere in the world comes to know Jesus." This statement is problematic. First and foremost, this statement is patently false no matter what dollar figure is attached to it. If this statement were true, then reaching the lost would be a simple mathematic equation. Once the church has given enough, everyone will be reached. But the reality is, it doesn't work that way. You might be able to give several thousand dollars, sponsor a preaching crusade in Latin America or East Africa, and see thousands attend and hundreds get saved. That would be a great investment! (I'm certainly not ever against the gospel being preached in this context.) But you could give the same amount of money to send missionaries to a place where no one has ever heard about Jesus, and they could spend *years* there before the first lost person follows Jesus. That also would be a great investment!

Our mission should be centered on and driven by bringing glory to God and our obedience to God's commission. When we understand these things, we are compelled to find the lost wherever they are and offer them restoration with their Creator. We should do more than count hands and keep score. We should care about more than the moment or the decision. We should not walk away from any believer until he or she is part of a healthy community of faith (church, house church, small group) that is discipling them and pushing them to reach those still lost in that region. This takes time. It takes investment. It involves process. And God is glorified in the process, not in the numbers.

This long view does not remove any urgency from our efforts to reach our lost neighbors, both near and far. In fact, it should increase our sense of urgency. Knowing that those who have yet to hear are in difficult or dangerous places and that connecting them to their Creator will take time and patience should cause us to redouble our efforts to give, pray, and go. The cause of global missions has never been more urgent, and it requires more patience, perseverance, and perspective than ever before.

"God is glorified in the process, not in the numbers."

This is a crude analogy, but in many ways, missions efforts amongst unreached peoples in difficult and dangerous places are similar to research and development in the pharmaceutical world. According to a recent study,[17] the process of developing a new prescription

---

[17] Taken from press released entitled "Cost to Develop and Win Marketing Approval for a New Drug Is $2.6 Billion" from Tufts Center for the Study of Drug Development on November 18, 2014.

drug from beginning to end (research, development, testing, FDA approval) is $2.6 billion dollars. Think of it this way: The first pill of any newly developed prescription drug costs the company $2.6 billion, while the second and every subsequent pill may cost only a few pennies to produce. Most of the hard work, expense, and risk goes into the creation of the first pill. Drug companies will seemingly spend whatever it takes to develop the next "new thing." Pioneer missions can seem like that some days. We have teams who have toiled away for years without a convert until, one day, sometimes after nearly a decade, the first plant begins to blossom. Followed by another and then another.

FINDING THE ONE

We lack understanding of the value of the process. We have become so "outcome based" that we've lost the ability, or maybe even the desire, to celebrate "the one." Jesus talked a lot about "the one" in Luke 15 through three parables: one lost sheep, one lost coin, one lost son. In each of these stories there is a *moment* when the *lost* one is *found*. But the stories are about much more than that moment. They are about the pursuit of the lost one. They are about the process of the lost being restored to found.

> So Jesus told them this story: "If a man has a hundred sheep and one of them gets lost, what will he do? Won't he leave the ninety-nine others in the wilderness and go to search for the one that is lost until he finds it? And when he has found it, he will joyfully carry it home on his shoulders. When he

arrives, he will call together his friends and neighbors, saying, 'Rejoice with me because I have found my lost sheep.' In the same way, there is more joy in heaven over one lost sinner who repents and returns to God than over ninety-nine others who are righteous and haven't strayed away!" (Luke 15:3–7)

Ninety-nine percent is exceptional in nearly any field. Ninety-nine percent in baseball will make you a Hall of Famer. Ninety-nine percent from the free throw line in basketball would make you the greatest free throw shooter in the history of the game. But 99 percent wasn't good enough for Jesus. He valued the one. Notice something: The one sheep apparently wasn't just lagging behind or lost around the corner or over the next hill. The sheep was *lost*. The shepherd wasn't content to send a search and rescue party. He went himself, and he went far away, *and*, get this, he left the 99! He searched for the lost one *until* he found it. There was a process in finding the sheep. The process was long enough that when the shepherd returned, he decided that a celebration was necessary.

"Or suppose a woman has ten silver coins and loses one. Won't she light a lamp and sweep the entire house and search carefully until she finds it? And when she finds it, she will call in her friends and neighbors and say, 'Rejoice with me because I have found my lost coin.' In the same way, there is joy in the presence of God's angels when even one sinner repents." (Luke 15:8–10)

We can all relate to a story about losing something. You name it, I've lost it.

Lost keys? Check.

Lost wallet? Check.

Lost cell phone? Check.

Lost car? Check.

We can all relate to losing things, but it can be difficult to fully appreciate the story of a lost coin in our Western context. Our coins today aren't worth much unless they're gold or centuries old. If you lost a coin on your way to work today, you likely wouldn't miss it or even backtrack to look for it. But this coin was important to this woman. The ten silver coins could have been her dowry, or even her entire life-savings, and ten percent of it was gone just like that. This was a personal and financial crisis of epic proportions. In addition to that stress, the flooring of her home would not have been tile, concrete, or dirt. The floor of her home was probably something like cobblestone—a series of large stones with smaller particles filling the gaps. When the coin fell, it could have hit a rounded edge of any stone in her floor and bounced in any direction. There was no guarantee of ever finding the coin. Literally thousands of crevices in her small home could have swallowed the coin forever. Similar to the lost sheep, there is a process here. She lit a lamp. She swept the house. She searched carefully *until* she found it.

To illustrate the point further, Jesus told them this story: "A man had two sons. The younger son told his father, 'I want my share of your estate now before you die.' So his father agreed to divide his wealth between his sons. A few days later this younger son packed all his belongings and moved to a distant land, and there he wasted all his money in wild living. About the time his money ran out, a great famine swept over the land, and he began to starve. He persuaded a local farmer to hire him, and the man sent him into his fields to feed the pigs. The young man became so hungry that even the pods he was feeding the pigs looked good to him. But no one gave him anything. When he finally came to his senses, he said to himself, 'At home even the hired servants have food enough to spare, and here I am dying of hunger! I will go home to my father and say, "Father, I have sinned against both heaven and you, and I am no longer worthy of being called your son. Please take me on as a hired servant."' So he returned home to his father. And while he was still a long way off, his father saw him coming. Filled with love and compassion, he ran to his son, embraced him, and kissed him. His son said to him, 'Father, I have sinned against both heaven and you, and I am no longer worthy of being called your son.' But his father said to the servants, 'Quick! Bring the finest robe in the house and put it on him. Get a ring for his finger and sandals for his feet. And kill the calf we have been fattening. We must celebrate with a feast, for this son of mine was dead and has now returned to life. He was lost, but now he is found.' So the party began." (Luke 15:11–24)

Once again, there is a *process* between *lost* and *found*. In this case, the process might have taken months or even years. The moment of restoration where the father embraced the son was months or years in the making.

"...there is a process between lost and found."

There's little doubt that early readers of this story associated the idea of a Hebrew son in a foreign land returning home with the story of the exile. Even though Israel was no longer in a geographic exile, many felt as though they lived in exile under foreign and pagan rule. "For Jesus to tell a story about a wicked son, lost in a foreign land, who was welcomed back with a lavish party—this was bound to be heard as a reference to the hope of Israel. 'This my son was dead, and is alive'; ever since Ezekiel 37 the idea of resurrection had been used as picture-language for the true return from exile."[18] Jesus was saying that the long wait was over! When people responded to the gospel, they were returning home from exile. And the God of the long view was waiting on the front

---

[18] N. T. Wright. *Luke for Everyone*. Louisville, KY: Westminster John Knox Press, 2004. 188.

porch to run and meet them, to welcome them home. The father had his long-lost son back, and he was worth the wait and worthy of celebration.

And so was Craig.

And so is the Chinese man in the mountains of the Yunnan Province.

And so is the secular woman in her apartment in Paris.

And so is the Muslim fundamentalist in West Africa.

And so is your neighbor.

Jesus told these stories because the religious people didn't understand why He hung out with and celebrated with all the wrong kinds of people. Still today, there is significant pushback from the "religious" people when the church engages with the lost with no regard to race, location, or current religion. If we stop reading Luke 15 at verse 24, we miss a huge point that Jesus was making:

> "Meanwhile, the older son was in the fields working. When he returned home, he heard music and dancing in the house, and he asked one of the servants what was going on. 'Your brother is back,' he was told, 'and your father has killed the fattened calf. We are celebrating because of his safe return.' The older brother was angry and wouldn't go in. His father

came out and begged him, but he replied, 'All these years I've slaved for you and never once refused to do a single thing you told me to. And in all that time you never gave me even one young goat for a feast with my friends. Yet when this son of yours comes back after squandering your money on prostitutes, you celebrate by killing the fattened calf!' His father said to him, 'Look, dear son, you have always stayed by me, and everything I have is yours. We had to celebrate this happy day. For your brother was dead and has come back to life! He was lost, but now he is found!'" (Luke 15:25–32)

Jesus made a very clear accusation against the religious elite, for they had lost the ability or desire to celebrate what God was celebrating. The lost "ones" no longer mattered to them. They were more interested in protecting their turf and getting what was "rightfully" theirs.

I am the older brother. I am the religious elite with a sense of entitlement. And there's probably a little bit of the older brother in all of us.

In terms of what God was doing in Israel through Jesus, we can see once more that the new kingdom-work which was going forward was indeed like a return from exile. Sinners and outcasts were finding themselves welcomed into fellowship with Jesus, and so with God, in a way they would have thought impossible. But whenever a work of God goes powerfully forwards, there is always someone muttering in the background that things aren't that easy, that God's got no right to be generous, that people who've done nothing wrong are being overlooked. That happened at the time when the exiles returned from Babylon; several people, not least the Samaritans, didn't want them back.[19]

The process and the time that it takes to move from lost to found can be long, painful, and ugly, but the question is this: When the Father runs after the younger brother, are we more likely to celebrate or grumble? Thankfully, the Father offers His grace just as freely to the religious older brother as He does to the reprobate younger brother. As for this "older brother," I want to celebrate the "one" *and* the "thousands" who come Jesus. And I'll continue in gratitude that the God of the long view sees not only past the reprobate's sins, but also past my self-righteousness.

---

[19] Ibid. 191.

CHAPTER 9

AN ANSWER TO PRAYER

"I want to tell you a growing conviction with me, and that is that as we obey the leadings of the Spirit of God, we enable God to answer the prayers of other people. I mean that our lives, **my life, is the answer to someone's prayer, prayed perhaps centuries ago.** *It is more and more impossible to me to have programs and plans because God alone has the plan, and our plans are only apt to hinder Him, and make it necessary for Him to break them up. I have the unspeakable knowledge that my life is the answer to prayers, and that God is blessing me and making me a blessing entirely of His sovereign grace and nothing to do with my merits, saving as I am bold enough to trust His leading and not the dictates of my own wisdom and common sense."*

OSWALD CHAMBERS (EMPHASIS MINE)

The God of the long view often works in ways we cannot see. We are limited to a time and a place, but our time and place do not confine God. Oswald Chambers held the firm conviction that his life was an answer to someone's prayer "prayed perhaps centuries ago," which makes the idea of the God of the long view not a new one. But what did Oswald Chambers mean when he said that?

The name Oswald Chambers may sound familiar as his devotional book *My Utmost for His Highest* is one of the best-selling devotional books of all time. What's fascinating is that Oswald Chambers didn't even write the book. It contains his words, sure enough, but all of his "writings" as published today were compiled by his wife Gertrude. (Chambers had a nickname for his wife; he called her "Biddy," short for "Beloved Disciple.") Biddy posthumously published the works of Oswald Chambers from notes she took while listening to her husband teach and preach.

Oswald Chambers moved from England to Cairo, Egypt, to serve as a YMCA chaplain during World War I. He died there at age 43 and is buried in the British War Cemetery in Cairo. I have visited his grave a number of times. It's marked with a simple marker that includes his name and date of death and the words: "A believer in Jesus Christ."

A short 5-minute walk from the cemetery where Chambers is buried is a cemetery in which another champion of the cross is buried. His name is William Whiting Borden. Borden came from a wealthy American family, and he abandoned the family fortune to follow God's call on his life. While attending Yale University, he was called to be a missionary in China. As Borden edged toward pursuing his call, he wrote a motto in his journal:

> **No Reserves.** Borden determined not to have a plan to fall back on. His family fortune could provide one, but he sought no backup plan.

> **No Retreats.** Once he left America, Borden knew he would likely never return. For him, retreat from God's call or God's plan was not an option.

> **No Regrets.** For Borden, regret was not part of the equation. He looked forward, not back.

Called to China as a missionary, Borden went to Cairo for training. Borden's aspirations to enter missions work in China never became reality as he died an untimely death at age 25 in Cairo. This son of privilege and wealth is buried in a commoner's grave in Cairo, just a few hundred yards from Oswald Chambers. Borden never reached China, but maybe in the same way Oswald Chambers was the answer to someone's prayer prayed centuries ago, someone today is serving as God's answer to William Borden's prayer to see the lost reached in China.

AN INCREDIBLE "COINCIDENCE"

Let me share one beautiful example of how a "long view" such as this can sometimes look in the work we do in difficult places. Consider this one example of how you might be the answer to someone's prayer centuries ago. The Yunnan Province is one of the most unreached places in China. It's really hard to get there. After a 14-hour flight to Beijing, we took a three-and-a-half-hour flight from Beijing to Kunming (a city the size of New York City but pretty much unheard of in America). From there, we took a bus for three hours into the mountains to a small town of around one million people. This town was remote, and our group of 16 Americans was the largest group of foreigners to ever visit. We met kids who had never seen a white person before.

Our organization started a coffee shop in this town. It's the only coffee shop in this town of one million people. Actually, it's the only foreign-owned business in town. There are no Dunkin Donuts, no Starbucks, no McDonald's. While this place is beyond the influence of the West, people are developing a taste for coffee. So they come, drink coffee, eat a slice of pizza, build relationships with our team, and get an opportunity to hear about Jesus. One young man rode two hours on a bus every day after school just to have coffee and hear about Jesus. Eventually, some friends bought him a scooter so he could make the trip in 30 minutes. He's now a believer in Jesus Christ, the first member of the first church God is building in this town.

Our workers on the ground desired to expand beyond this town into the surrounding villages, and one local mentioned that surrounding the town in the mountains of the Yunnan Province were coffee plantations. How could this be? How could there be coffee plantations in a place where the local people don't even drink coffee? After a little research, our workers found this information to be true and discovered that the Yunnan Province grows 90 percent of all coffee beans in China. Starbucks even recently released a Yunnan coffee blend.

In China, visitors cannot just go wherever they want. In every town I visited, I had to present my passport to the local police to be registered. Authorities are always watching. Thus, the workers cannot just go evangelizing through the mountains. They must have a reason to be there, and they have to register when they arrive. But now, because we know coffee beans are grown in these villages, we have a reason to go! We now buy coffee beans from them.

But how exactly did people who don't *drink* coffee come to *grow* coffee? Enter the God of the long view. In 1852, a French missionary named Pere Charles Renou came to the mountains of the Yunnan Province. He came to build the church among the Yi people there.

He built a few buildings which survive today, but otherwise he had very little success in building anything that lasted. There are no churches and no believers in those mountains.[20]

But Renou brought the gospel and something else with him—two coffee plants. He loved coffee, so he brought plants to grow in order to harvest beans, roast them, and brew coffee for himself. Upon arrival, he found the mountainous environment perfect for growing coffee, so he taught the locals about the coffee trade and showed them how to grow coffee for export. One of the two original coffee plants brought by this French missionary is still alive and producing beans today. If you haven't put it together yet, here's what's amazing: God sent a French missionary 166 years ago to a region of China where coffee didn't exist so that our workers could have legitimate access to hundreds of thousands of people working in the coffee trade in those mountain villages today. If that missionary had not gone, there would be no coffee growing in the region, leaving our team with no access to the area, leaving multitudes of people with no opportunity to hear about Jesus. That's the God of the long view.

Can God ordain and anoint a business to help plant the church? What do you think? If we started an English center, a gym, a tour

---

[20] I heard the story of Pere Charles Renou firsthand from farmers in the coffee plantations and our team in the Yunnan Province. Former church buildings and other local records identify Renou. I also found more information by searching Charles Renou on the Mission-Thibet website: http://mission-thibet.org.

company, a restaurant, or anything else in this town, we would have no access to those villages. We would have no reason to be there. *But we started a coffee shop.* I believe the God of the long view knew that the only way for us to gain access to those villages in the 21st century was to send a French missionary 166 years earlier to teach the people how to grow coffee. Such an incredible "coincidence" that, in fact, is not a coincidence has led to the start of another business. Because we now buy raw beans in the mountains around town, we needed to open a coffee roasting business. That coffee roaster has its own location, its own visas, and its own employees and customers.

GOD'S ENDGAME

The God of the long view is growing His Church through businesses. Our team leader's wife in China met a young lady, whose English name is Lucky, at the store. Lucky told the leader's wife that she was the first white person and the first Christian she had ever met. Our worker became better acquainted with Lucky and talked to her about Jesus. Many times, Lucky said that Jesus was nice for Americans, but that He wasn't for her.

Our team leaders were expecting a baby and they felt strongly that God wanted them to deliver their baby in the town where He called them to serve. When the time came for the baby to be delivered, a Western midwife was brought in and Lucky came to help her American friends. Things didn't go well. The baby was born without incident, but shortly after the baby's birth, the mother began to hemorrhage. There was no hospital in this town, and the nearest good healthcare was a day's travel away. The Western midwife was helpless with no knowledge of the local language; everything fell on Lucky to try to help. The midwife said they needed medication and an IV or the new mom would not survive. Lucky called everyone she knew. Everyone said no. What she asked just wasn't possible in China, it wasn't done.

After several phone calls, the situation became more and more desperate—our team member was bleeding to death. Lucky decided to do something she had never done before. She stopped to pray. She prayed to the God that she heard her American friends pray to. She asked God to intervene and help her. She picked up the phone and called a man who had already told her no. But this time his answer was different. He said he would come. He would bring the medication. He would bring an IV. Our team member's life was spared, and for the first time in her life, Lucky thought that maybe, just maybe, the God *of the Americans* wasn't just *for the Americans*. A few weeks later, our team members returned to the States for further medical treatment, and while they were there, Lucky walked into our coffee shop, and amidst the burr of the coffee grinder and steam of the espresso machine, a team member led her in a prayer to ask Jesus into her heart. Lucky is the second member of the first church God is building in this town.

There was no evidence of lasting fruit from his missionary life in the Yunnan Province, so Pere Charles Renou may have died feeling like a failure. I'm guessing he didn't feel like the answer to anyone's prayer. But he was on the opposite side of Oswald Chamber's prayer equation. Rather than being the answer to a prayer centuries later, he was praying the prayer centuries before. Perhaps we are the answer to someone's prayer prayed centuries ago or maybe we are praying the prayer that someone will answer centuries from now.

Like many missionaries in difficult places, Pere Charles Renou must have prayed a prayer that God's Church would be built on the mountains of the Yunnan Province. Today, God is answering that prayer through a team of believers making coffee for their Chinese friends. God is restoring the Yi people to Himself. One at a time. One day at a time. A century at a time. A millennium at a time. It's all the same to the God of the long view. Prayers don't often work like microwaves or Amazon Prime. You can't click a button and pay three more dollars for afternoon delivery. You can't push a button and "zap" the work of God into someone's life in mere seconds.

> *"Perhaps we are the answer to someone's prayer prayed centuries ago or maybe we are praying the prayer that someone will answer centuries from now."*

His endgame is not tied to your lifetime. His endgame started with the *protoevangelium*, with the first gospel in Genesis. He's coming after you. He's doing the long, drawn-out work of restoring humanity to Himself. He's finding gold in streets of dirt. He's building His Church. And this work is an answer to many prayers prayed over centuries and millennia.

CHAPTER 10

SILK, SAND & STONE

"Wait on God and He will work, but don't wait in spiritual sulks because you cannot see an inch in front of you! Are we detached enough from our spiritual hysterics to wait on God? To wait is not to sit with folded hands, but to learn to do what we are told."

OSWALD CHAMBERS

This long restoration between God and humanity is just that—long. It's so long, in fact, that many times the progress seems glacially slow from our perspective. There's a cornfield near my house that I walk past when I exercise. There are two times each year when I can see progress from one day to the next: the day the farmer plows the field and the day he harvests. In between, the progress from day to day is not all that visible. If I travel for a week and come back, then I can see the corn has grown. Cognitively, I know the crop grows every day, but I can't see it growing. God's global Kingdom, His pursuit of humanity is often the same way, but on a macro scale.

"You are probably too close to see what God is doing."

If you are a pastor, doing the day-to-day work of the church, you may not see growth from one day to the next. In fact, you are more likely to notice damage to the crops than you are to see daily growth. If you are missionary, particularly in a dangerous or difficult context, you probably don't see the Kingdom growing from one day to the next. Here's my word of encouragement to you both: You are probably too close to see what God is doing.

A SILKWORM SAW?

In Istanbul, there is a beautiful building called the Hagia Sophia. The first Hagia Sophia was built in the 4th century largely by Constantinius II (even though some credit Constantine the Great with starting construction) who upon its completion patted himself on the back and declared it the most beautiful building ever built. A few years after its completion, it burned to the ground. The only remnant of original building is the stone baptismal. Theodosius II then began construction of the second version in the early 5th century, and that second Hagia Sophia lasted 115 years before it also burned down. In the year 532, just a few weeks after the second fire, Emperor Justinian I began construction of a bigger, better church on the same grounds. He decided that this time there would be no wood in the structure. The building burned twice already, and he wanted this final version to last. Over 10,000 people were involved in the construction of this third church. The massive number of tradespeople involved led to the completion of the exterior of this massive structure in just under six years, although work on the interior continued for several more years, including breathtaking gold mosaics that cover the interior.

The Hagia Sophia has a fascinating history beyond its multiple constructions. It was first an Orthodox cathedral. After the invasion of the Crusaders in the 13th century, it became a Roman Catholic cathedral. Once the Ottomans conquered Constantinople (now Istanbul) in the 15th century, it was transformed into a mosque. When it became a mosque, all the mosaics and Christian symbols were plastered, painted, or covered with cloth. In the early 20th century, the building became a "museum," and today, it's an odd hybrid of half Muslim mosque and half Christian cathedral. The work to remove plaster and reveal portions of the original beauty of the mosaics is ongoing as curators try to strike a balance in preserving the building's diverse history.

Through all the changes of "management," one thing has remained the same over the centuries. One thing was not covered in plaster. One thing has not led to arguments between Muslims and Christians—the floors. The floors are original and largely preserved, and they date all the way back to the 6th century.

The floors are a beautiful marble. I've toured many cathedrals and churches around the world, but I've never seen anything quite like these floors. They are comprised of large slabs or tiles of marble arranged in such a way that where they join together, the pattern in the marble flows continually from one piece to another. They are truly stunning. And I knew they were beautiful, but I did not understand how difficult creating this beauty was until my tour guide, Omar, explained. In order for the pattern to flow from one piece of marble to the next, the craftsmen had to "slice off" very thin slabs (an inch or less) from a larger piece. They took these thin slabs and flipped them back and forth so the grain matched up.

As he explained it, I became even more impressed, but Omar saw that I had not yet fully understood. He reminded me that this work was done 1,500 years ago and he asked me how I would have done it if I were a marble craftsman of the 6th century. (Omar could not have understood how ironic this question was for me as I am not a craftsman of any kind.) A saw, I thought. I would use some kind of saw. Omar explained that a saw wouldn't work for three reasons: (1) The saw would remove too much material between the slabs for the patterns to align properly; (2) the saw would leave the surface of the marble much too rough; and (3) the saw would create too much vibration and cause the thin piece of marble to break off before each slice could be completed.

I was at a loss and Omar knew it. He let me off the hook and gave me the answer: silk, sand, and olive oil. OK, makes sense... Wait. What? Omar continued, explaining that the process of creating these beautiful thin slabs of marble for the floors of the Hagia Sophia (and even some of the walls) involved craftsmen using thin strips of silkworm silk, olive oil for lubrication, and sand as an abrasive. They cut giant slabs of thin marble with silk, sand, and olive oil? Apparently.

Imagine the first construction meeting when the lead craftsman says, "Yeah, uh, hey, guys, I have an idea on cutting those thin stone slabs."

"We're listening."

"I think we should use silk."

Crickets.

"Well, not *just* silk. We would need a little sand, too."

More crickets.

"Oh, and olive oil. We'll need *lots* of olive oil."

Imagine the first demonstration of the process—sawing back and forth with taut twisted strands of silk on a slab of marble, wondering if it was going to actually cut?

As one might imagine, this was a painfully slow process. The average craftsman made about two millimeters of progress every day (about a tenth of an inch).

Silk. Sand. Olive oil. Marble.

Back and forth. Back and forth. Back and forth.

A tenth of an inch today.

Almost an inch by the week's end.

Nearly three inches by the end of the month.

Silk. Sand. Olive oil. Marble.

Back and forth. Back and forth. Back and forth.

Three feet of progress this year.

After two years of work, one panel was finally cut.

Hundreds of craftsmen did the same work. Imagine this being your life.

"What do you do for a living?"

"Oh, I take a piece of silkworm silk and a little bit of sand and olive oil and rub it back and forth on a piece of marble."

"For how long?"

"I've been doing it for a year and a half and I have yet to cut off my first piece."

"How long will it take?"

"I don't know. I guess 'til it's done."

I can't imagine the monotony of that process. Silk. Sand. Olive oil. Marble. Day after day after day. I can't imagine the discouragement of such little progress.

The craftsman had a choice. He could focus on the monotony of the task. He could choose frustration because progress is so slow. He could choose irritation because the process wasn't better. Or he could step back and choose to see the "little" thing he was doing was part of an architect's bigger plan. That thin, frustratingly-slow-to-cut slab of marble is a piece of a very beautiful plan. The craftsman could choose to "zoom out" and see that without his work, the greater work would never be completed.

We have that same choice. Progress advancing the Kingdom of God in my little corner of the world can seem frustratingly slow at times. For some of our workers in difficult or dangerous places, it is even slower. Glacially

> **"We can choose frustration, discouragement, fear of failure, or many other things. Or we can choose to trust the Architect."**

slow. We can work years before we see the first signs of the silk beginning to cut into the stone. Day after day. Week after week. Year after year.

We can choose frustration, discouragement, fear of failure, or many other things. Or we can choose to trust the Architect. We can choose to zoom out and see the big picture of what it is we are participants in building. We can choose to trust the plan and keep sawing away.

Silk. Sand. Olive oil. Marble.

In this long restoration, God calls many partners to work with Him in restoring humanity into relationship with Himself. Partners in the West. Partners in the East. Partners in the First World. Partners in the developing world. Partners in difficult places. Partners in relatively "easy" places. And right now, we all have one job.

Keep cutting.

Silk. Sand. Olive oil. Marble.

But I'm not seeing any growth in my church.

Keep sawing.

Silk. Sand. Olive oil. Marble.

But I feel further from God than I did at one time in my life.

Keep sawing.

Silk. Sand. Olive oil. Marble.

But I've been in this country for seven years and we've only baptized one new believer.

Keep sawing.

Silk. Sand. Olive oil. Marble.

You might be too close to see the corn growing, but it is. Soon, it will be harvest time.

How long do we work?

Until it's finished. "So we must not get tired of doing good, for we will reap at the proper time if we don't give up" (Gal. 6:9 HCSB).

Be patient with the process. Trust the plan. Trust the Architect. God chose to use us in this time and this place. We must zoom out and see the big picture every now and then—or hop aboard our imaginary 747s and see what God is doing from 30,000 feet. Because He is building His Church, and she sure is beautiful.

CHAPTER 11

A GRAVE, WALL & CROSS

"You have paralyzed all that is inside,
All that is the heart of this desperate man.
I will celebrate the coming of your love.
I can hardly wait for that glorious day.
Though I can't see you. Though I can't touch you.
I know that you are reaching out your hand.
I will always walk in your beauty.
When I cannot see your hand I'll trust your heart.
I can barely breath. I can hardly speak.
I can only close my eyes I can't even think.
You're all around me. You're all that I can see.
The closer that I get the more I am free.
I believe in miracles.
I believe in the God that saved the Universe.
To live this life without you, I could think of nothing worse."

JEFF ANDERSON

I'm sensing a trend here that many of my stories begin in some old, dusty church. Well, here's another one. One of my favorite spots in London is Westminster Abbey. It's a beautiful, old church right next to Big Ben and the Palace of Westminster where the British Parliament meets. One of the "things to do" at Westminster Abbey is to locate the graves of the many famous people buried there. Seventeen British monarchs are buried there including Henry V. Isaac Newton is buried in Westminster Abbey. The abbey is also the final resting place of Charles Dickens. They're all in good company. Over 3,000 people are buried in Westminster Abbey. But when I visited, I was only interested in finding the final resting place of one person: David Livingstone. His body is interred at Westminster Abbey—well, most of it anyway.

ISLAND PROPERTY GIVEN

Livingstone was a pioneer missionary to Africa. His is a great story that's been told by credible biographers.[21] I won't try to retell a

---

[21] See Martin Dugard's *Into Africa: The Epic Adventures of Stanley and Livingstone* or Janet and Geoff Benge's *David Livingstone: Africa's Trailblazer*.

story that others tell much better than I could, but I'd like to pick up the story of Livingstone where many biographers conclude it. Livingstone has been re-characterized and reclassified by many as an adventurer and a missionary. This is revisionist at best. While Livingstone certainly had his adventures in Africa, and he is credited with many discoveries geographical and otherwise, any characterization of his life and work as anything other than overt missionary efforts to spread the good news about Jesus on the continent are misguided at best, and intentionally misleading at worst. Dr. Livingstone went to Africa to tell people about Jesus. He first felt a call to China but was later greatly influenced by Robert Moffat who told him of a place in Africa where he had seen "the smoke of a thousand villages, where no missionary had ever been." So Dr. Livingstone went. He is revered as a great missionary—and rightfully so. He took to the gospel to places it had never been.

Our modern imagination of what it might have looked like is very different from the reality. We imagine the great missionary Dr. Livingstone traveling from village to village and leaving in his wake a church in every town, a baptized believer in every home. But the reality of Dr. Livingstone's missionary endeavors is far from that. In reality, Dr. Livingstone only ever successfully converted one African to faith in Christ. Dr. Livingstone's lone convert was a man name Sechele. In reality, Dr. Livingstone's endeavors to evangelize the lost in unreached and unengaged Africa look very similar to the efforts of my friends working among the unreached in places like Somalia, Sudan, and Saudi Arabia today: a lifetime of ministry for one convert. Was Dr. Livingstone a failure? Of course not. Like his contemporary Pere Charles Renou in the mountains of the Yunnan province in China, Dr. Livingstone was praying a prayer that would be answered over the next century and a half.

Dr. Livingstone's one convert became a missionary himself. Sechele took the gospel to surrounding villages so effectively that when European missionaries came in after Livingstone they "astonishingly found that the tribe already had regular Christian prayers."[22] Sechele traveled hundreds of miles teaching, preaching, praying, and singing. Neil Parsons of the University of Botswana surmises that Sechele "did more to propagate Christianity in nineteenth-century southern Africa than virtually any single European missionary."[23] This is what an indigenous church planting movement should look like from a missiological point of view. Even though every pastor, missionary, or even Christian probably likes to imagine themselves as a Paul, we are actually called to be Barnabas. Our job is to find our Paul or our Sechele—an indigenous leader with an apostolic gifting who can do more than we ever could.

But Dr. Livingstone's story doesn't end with Sechele. Dr. Livingstone died on May 1, 1873, in what is known today as Zambia. His porters, Chuma and Susi, removed his heart and intestines and buried them

---

[22] Stephen Tomkins. *David Livingstone: The Unexplored Story.* 235.
[23] Ibid. 236.

under a tree near the place he died. After they commemorated him with both a Christian reading and an African tribal drum ceremony, they carefully packed the rest of his body with salt to preserve it and wrapped it in bark, cloth, and tar. They then carried it over 1,000 miles to the eastern coast of Africa to a town called Bagamoyo. From there they waited for the tides to cooperate, so his body could be taken to the island of Zanzibar. The journey took nine months. From there, the Anglican church relieved Chuma and Susi of their duties and took Dr. Livingstone's body to Westminster for a proper British burial. Chuma and Susi had travelled months through wild animal-infested territory to deliver Dr. Livingstone safely to the Anglicans. Chuma and Susi received a fair payment from the Anglican church, but they also learned they had been deeded a piece of property on Zanzibar by Dr. Livingstone himself. It was their honor to serve their friend, Dr. Livingstone. Chuma and Susi never inhabited the island property and the deed fell back to the Anglican church. This piece of property sat vacant in the hands of the Anglican church for over 120 years. Aside from a few graves, nothing about the land changed for over a century.

ISLAND PROPERTY PURCHASED

Fast forward 122 years. The missionary efforts initiated by Livingstone and the London Missionary Society have blossomed into a movement of indigenous churches across Africa. Supported by missionaries from many countries and many agencies, these national churches are some of the strongest indigenous churches anywhere in the world. My friend, Pastor Dixon Kikonga, is a product of one of these national churches. He is a powerful preacher, a gifted teacher, and a talented musician. In the mid-1990s, Dixon began to hear God calling him to the island of Zanzibar. Today, Zanzibar is 99 percent Muslim. In 1995, there were no strong evangelical or Pentecostal churches in Stone Town (the old part of Zanzibar City, the main city on the island of Zanzibar in Tanzania). So, like Dr. Livingstone before him, Pastor Dixon decided to take the gospel where it wasn't. In the latter half of 1995, a gathering of Tanzania missionaries took place at a location called Mtoni Marina. My friend Greg Beggs (then field director for Tanzania and today the Regional Director for AGWM Africa) was in that meeting. While the missionaries were meeting, Pastor Dixon interrupted them. He had been trying to acquire a piece of property on which to build a church in Stone Town. Because the area was mostly controlled by Muslims, no one wanted to sell him property to build a church, so he had roamed through town just looking for undeveloped land.

One parcel he happened upon was the parcel that the Anglican church received via Chuma, Susi, and Dr. Livingstone, which was vacant for over 120 years. Squatters had now pushed in on the land. When Pastor Dixon inquired as to the land ownership, he was told the Anglican church owned it. Pastor Dixon met with the local Anglican officials and offered to buy it. The answer was clear: "It's not for sale." Just as Pastor Dixon was about to leave the office, the Anglican official said, "But...." Wait for it. "But we will give it to you to build your church on two conditions: You must agree to receive it as it is because it's a graveyard and you must build a wall around the perimeter to protect against squatters and so that the neighbors who are Muslim won't have to look at your church."

Pastor Dixon raced to the meeting of missionaries he knew was happening on the island to share the news. As he and Greg stepped outside the meeting, Pastor Dixon said, "You know, missionary, we've been looking for a piece of land for years and years and years. You know all the trouble we've had and the places we've been kicked out of. You know that it's impossible to start a church with no land." He said, "We've been offered a piece of land from the Anglican church on two conditions. We have to accept that it's a graveyard. There's some land that doesn't have any graves where we can build, but we have to accept that it's a graveyard. And second, we have to build a wall." Pastor Dixon continued, "Missionary, I'm OK with the graveyard, but I have no money to build a wall." The land was free, but the wall would cost approximately $40,000. For Pastor Dixon, the cost might as well have been $40 million. The cost of the wall was a dream killer. He didn't have it and he couldn't get it. Greg returned to the meeting and reported the opportunity to the rest of the missionaries there. The land was free, but the wall would cost $40,000. The missionaries in the room that day raised the $40,000 to build the wall around the property. The deed was transferred, and the wall was built. Today, there is a vibrant, missions-minded church meeting on that property.

It hasn't been easy. Early on, the neighbors threw rocks onto the tin roof of the building to make noise to disrupt the worship. On

Christmas Day 2008, there was a failed bombing attempt. Late one night in 2012, some local youth breached the wall of the church property and gathered everything combustible and burned it, including Pastor Dixon's car. It hasn't been an easy road, but the gospel is being preached in Stone Town. The lost are being reached in Stone Town. Every Sunday, Pastor Dixon preaches the gospel to the largest gathering of Christ-followers ever assembled on the island. Recent years have brought even more hardship. In 2017, the Kikonga family suffered a terrible tragedy when Pastor Dixon's 21-year-old son slipped and fell in the shower and died soon after from a catastrophic head injury. No one ever said being the answer to someone's prayer would be easy.

> *"No one ever said being the answer to someone's prayer would be easy."*

Just a few kilometers from Pastor Dixon's church is another church in Stone Town, an Anglican cathedral called Christ Church. Its construction began just a few months after David Livingstone died in 1873. As a matter of fact, the foundation stone was laid on December 25, 1873, just 60 days or so before Dr. Livingstone's body passed through the island on its way to England. Today in that church hangs a wooden cross. The cross is not ornate or decorative. It's not a cross that would grab your attention. What's unique about the cross is the origin of the wood from which it's fashioned. The cross that hangs in Christ Church Stone Town in Zanzibar is made from the tree under which Dr. Livingstone's heart was buried.

Over 145 years since the passing of David Livingstone, the missionary with one convert has at least a symbolic, if not significant, presence in two churches on one tiny island. The story of David Livingstone's impact is, of course, not limited to Stone Town. There are literally hundreds of churches and perhaps tens of thousands of Christ-followers on the continent of Africa who can trace their spiritual heritage to the moment David Livingstone decided to follow the smoke to the villages where people had never heard the gospel. I wonder if Dr. Livingstone felt like a success or a failure. I think he was like many of us who are sawing away at marble with silkworm silk and sand. My guess is, there were moments he doubted his effectiveness. Likely there were moments he wondered if he was making a difference and moments he worried that no one would remember his work. But now, in many places across Africa, there are memorials to the missionary who came before any others.

Today in Stone Town, Bishop Dixon Kikonga is the answer to the prayers that Dr. Livingstone prayed almost a century and a half ago. If you want to go back even further into history, perhaps Dr. Livingstone was the answer to prayers that the Gospel writer and evangelist John Mark prayed. Mark was one of the first believers and almost certainly the first disciple of Jesus to step foot on the continent of Africa. About two decades after Jesus ascended to heaven, Mark landed in Alexandria, Egypt. He became the first bishop of the church he founded in Alexandria, and he is widely regarded as the pioneer or founder of Christianity in Africa.

The prayers that John Mark prayed for the nascent church in Africa were answered by Dr. Livingstone and Bishop Kikonga and they continue to be answered by thousands of Kingdom workers across the continent. Mark's prayers are even being answered today in the town he lived in almost 2,000 years ago. In Alexandria, mosques and crescent moons that dot the horizon stamped out or covered much of the Christian heritage founded by  Mark. Still, in the midst of the prayer calls that ring out across this beautiful city on the Mediterranean, there is a multi-national team of workers building the Church among local Egyptians. My friends in Alexandria could not build a Western style church with a steeple and pews (building or renovating a church in Egypt is against the law), so they built a CrossFit gym. Every day local Egyptians come to work out, and while at the gym, they hear the good news about Jesus. And slowly, but ever so surely, in Alexandria the God of the long view is building His Church and answering prayers prayed centuries ago.

CHAPTER 12

FAR FROM HOME

"A certain man once lost a diamond cuff-link in the wide blue sea, and twenty years later, on the exact day, a Friday apparently, he was eating a large fish—but there was no diamond inside. That's what I like about coincidence."

VLADIMIR NABOKOV

It's difficult to describe how far Mbeya, Tanzania is from my home in Bloomington, Indiana. There really is no easy way to get there:

- A one-hour drive to the Indianapolis airport
- A one-hour flight to Detroit
- Eight hours to Schiphol Airport in Amsterdam
- Ten more hours south by plane to Dar Es Salaam, Tanzania
- Finally, 14 more hours on a very underdeveloped Tanzanian highway system to Mbeya

Mbeya is just a few kilometers from the borders of Zambia and Malawi in the southwest corner of Tanzania. On any given day, any American in Mbeya is likely the only American in Mbeya, unless two Americans are traveling together.

In June 2013, I went to Mbeya, Tanzania at the invitation of my friend Rev. Dr. Barnabas Mtokambali to speak at a special dedication of a church planting school situated a couple of hours away in an even more remote, out-of-the-way town called Makambako. Tanzania's culture is one of honor and as such, while I was there, I had a "driver" to take me around to the various meetings, meals, and services. My driver during my three days there was a man I had never met before whose name was Pastor George James.

Pastor George is a quiet man with a very sweet spirit. He gave his heart to Christ in 1988. Eight years later he felt called by God to become a full-time minister. He went to Bible college and completed his education, and after pastoring for a couple of years, Pastor George became the principal of the Bible college in Mbeya. You don't have to spend much time with Pastor George to see that he has the heart of a teacher and a mentor. He lives on the college campus with his wife and two children, and he mentors, coaches, educates, and trains dozens of men and women who are preparing themselves for full-time ministry. Over the last ten years, Pastor George has helped to train hundreds of men and women for ministry.

I spent three days getting in and out of Pastor George's late-1990s Toyota Cressida, and he says it was there the whole time, but I never saw it until my very last ride with him on my way to the airport after the conference. I saw on the armrest between the driver and passenger seats a burgundy leather Bible. Something about the Bible caught my attention—a name stamped in gold foil on its cover. This struck me as odd for a couple of reasons. Having a name stamped on a Bible is a fairly distinctly American thing. I've never seen it anywhere else in the world. I didn't research this, but I've been to Tanzania about 15 times, and I doubt there's anywhere in the entire country with the capability to stamp names in gold foil on Bibles. It also struck me as odd because it seemed out of character for this simple, quiet man of God to have his name stamped on his Bible in gold leaf. Then I noticed something. It wasn't his name. My eyes focused on the gold foil stamping in the lower right-hand corner of that burgundy NIV Thinline Bible. I was still a little jet-lagged and worn down emotionally, physically, and spiritually from three days of preaching, so were my eyes playing tricks on me? No, that can't be right. YES, that's what it says: *Karen Cooper.*

I had the sense that something special was happening when I asked Pastor George where and how he got the Bible. He said, "A few years ago, a friend of mine was travelling to Dar Es Salaam, so I gave him some schillings and asked him to try to find me a NIV Bible." Pastor George speaks and reads very good English. Many of the classes he teaches at the Bible college are taught in English. Until 2004, all he had was a Swahili Bible and King James Version Bible. So, almost ten years before, he sent some money with a friend who was going to the "big city" to buy him a NIV Bible. That friend found this Bible at a used bookstore in Dar Es Salaam, Tanzania. He paid 1,500 schillings for it—about one U.S. dollar. Since the fall of 2004, Pastor George says that Bible has been his constant companion to every Bible college class he taught, every chapel service he preached, and every Sunday morning service he attended or led. He said he loves it because it's indexed, he can always find his place.

So how does a Bible with the name of my lifelong friend and brother-in-law's mother end up in Pastor George's hands in Mbeya, Tanzania? Coincidence? Needle in a haystack? Happenstance? The God of the long view! Providence! Albert Einstein once mused that maybe "coincidence is God's way of remaining anonymous." Karen remembers donating several Bibles to a "Bible Drive" at our local

church in Indianapolis nearly 25 years ago. She wasn't going to donate ones with her name on them or ones with keepsake value, but she remembers her father-in-law Rev. Ed Cooper saying, "Karen, Bibles weren't meant to be kept as keepsakes on a shelf gathering dust. They were meant to be used." So she gave it. And right about the time Pastor George was leaving a life of tribal religion, animism, and witchcraft and giving his life to Jesus thousands of miles away, Karen Cooper gave a few Bibles. One of those Bibles ended up in a used bookstore in Dar Es Salaam. After more than 20 years, she had nearly forgotten it and certainly didn't know where any of those Bibles ended up. Interestingly, the one thing Karen remembers for sure about this particular Bible is that she gave it away because she didn't like the indexing—the very thing that Pastor George loves about the Bible.

"So will the words that come out of my mouth not come back empty-handed. They'll do the work I sent them to do, they'll complete the assignment I gave them" (Isa. 55:11 MSG).

On a dusty road in Mbeya, Tanzania, in 2013, I got a little glimpse of heaven. Can you imagine what it will be like when the curtains that separate us from eternity's perspective are rolled back and we see all the investments we made in the Kingdom of God? Can you imagine the infinite number of ways the God of the long view is weaving together our stories for His glory?

> *"Can you imagine the infinite number of ways the God of the long view is weaving together our stories for His glory?"*

CHAPTER 13

JOY IN THE WAITING ROOM

"One can never consent to creep when one feels an impulse to soar."

HELEN KELLER

Do you remember doctors' waiting rooms when you were a kid? You walked into the doctor's office and up to the sliding glass window and then watched mom or dad sign in. In the days before HIPAA,[24] you saw the names of everyone in front of you, and if you were fast enough, you could count how many names were ahead of you. Then you sat down and waited for the next person on the list to be called in to see the pediatrician. You watched the clock and calculated that it took 20 minutes for the first person to be called. Doing a little math, you figured out that by the time your name was called, you would be too old to see a pediatrician.

The wait felt like an eternity. "Kids these days" don't know how good they have it. Today, there are televisions in the waiting room and every kid I know has some sort of electronic device—an iPad, iPhone, Nintendo Switch. *When I was a kid*, there were no TVs or toys in the waiting room. There were magazines (usually about stuff I didn't care about) and hardcover children's books all written

---

[24] The Health Insurance Portability and Accountability Act (HIPAA)

for an audience of 2-year-olds. Figuring out what to do in the waiting room was one of my greatest childhood dilemmas (I lived a sheltered life).

I still struggle with waiting. I've been known to drive *miles* out of my way to avoid waiting at a train crossing even if I *know without a doubt* that I would arrive at my destination faster by waiting. I hate to wait. (Great, the guy writing the book about waiting on the God of the long view confesses three-fourths of the way through the book that he is terrible at waiting. Stay with me.) I don't think I'm alone, though. I think we all struggle with this in some way. Once a wait passes our 8-second attention span, we feel like it's been "forever." There are no magazines, televisions, or iPads in the waiting room of life. So what do you do while you wait? What do you do while you wait for your name to be called?

WAIT FOR JOY

I will not be the first, the last, or the most eloquent person to opine on the differences between happiness and joy. If you've been in church for a minute or two, you've likely heard a preacher talk about the difference between these two pursuits. But because God's actions in the long view often require us to wait, I feel the need to talk some about how to find joy in that waiting room.

Happiness and joy are not the same thing, but they are related. I believe that joy is worth pursuing and that joy can give birth to some happiness in your life. Joy is deep and abiding. Happiness is fleeting.

The confusion between the two could be that they evoke similar feelings in us, and we use those feelings to equate happiness with joy.

I love golf. I love to get out and walk the course. The feeling of hitting a great shot or sinking a birdie putt keeps me coming back. A few years ago, a friend invited me to try out a golf simulator. It was the dead of Indiana winter and the "golf itch" started to hit me pretty bad, so I thought, "Why not?" We took our clubs to a local establishment that recently opened. The proprietor set us up in our bay and turned on the projection screen and computer that controlled the hi-tech simulator.

"You can play any course you want to play," he said. "How about Pebble Beach? How about St. Andrews?"

I have played both courses and knew they were exceptional, so I said that either one was fine. The screen in front of us starting loading, and the message read, "Prepare to tee off on hole number one at Pebble Beach." We grabbed our clubs and off we went (not really, you stand in the same place the whole time). We hit a few shots and marveled at the graphics and technology. A series of cameras in the room picked up the speed and rotation of the ball in the 15 feet between where I hit the ball and where it made contact with the screen. When the real golf ball hit the screen with *thwack* and came to an abrupt stop, an animated version of the ball appeared on the screen and showed the remainder of the shot. The camera relocated on the course to show you where your ball landed so you could select a club and hit the next shot. The technology was amazing. It was even pretty accurate. But there was one thing it was not: actual *golf*. It was a golf simulator after all. It simulated golf. It was not the real thing. I still hit a ball, and I still saw the hole in front of me. But something was missing—authenticity. It just wasn't the same as the real thing.

I've never been in one, but I've heard the same thing about the incredibly expensive simulators used to train fighter pilots. These simulators are suspended in a large steel frame that allows movement so as the pilot takes a hard turn, she feels the effects of that turn on her body. Again, the technology is incredible, like the golf simulator, and it does a great job at simulating flight, but something is still missing—that almost intangible element of authenticity. Something still tells us that as we look at an incredibly accurate screen, this is not the real thing.

Tom Bodett, when he wasn't busy leaving a light on for you, said: "They say a person needs just three things to be truly happy in this world: someone to love, something to do, and something to hope for." Happiness is awesome. I love seeing people happy. I love working with happy people. I love making my wife and kids happy. But here's the thing: *Happiness is awesome, but happiness is at best a "joy simulator."* You can experience some of the same feelings. There may even be moments when you get the two confused. But happiness is not joy. It's missing that intangible element of authenticity. Happiness is circumstance- or feeling-driven. Your circumstances can make you happy. Money can help make you happy (despite the common cliché that says otherwise). Happiness is good. There's only one thing wrong with happiness: it's not joy.

Pierre Teilhard de Chardin said, "Joy is the infallible sign of the presence of God." The psalmist David seemed to have remarkable joy even when his circumstances were less than ideal. Chased by the king, hiding in a cave, fearing for his life, David had joy: "When I said, 'My foot is slipping,' your unfailing love, Lord, supported me. When anxiety was great within me, your consolation brought me joy" (Psalm 94:18–19 NIV). Happiness comes and goes. Joy comes and stays. Happiness is affected by circumstances. Joy comes in spite of horrible circumstances. You can pursue happiness. Joy is given to you.

> **"Happiness is awesome, but happiness is at best a 'joy simulator.'"**

After that first time, I never went back to the golf simulator. It just didn't feel right. I waited a few more weeks for the winter weather to break and I went to enjoy the real thing. Why would I ever settle for a simulation?

WHY WOULD YOU SETTLE

Why would you settle for the pursuit of happiness when incredible joy is available? Why would you crawl when you are made to soar? Why would you sit in a simulator when you could be pulling actual G's at 35,000 feet? We make this compromise in other areas, too. We settle for KFC when we could have Chick-fil-A. We settle for Whataburger when we could have In-N-Out, etc. We trade God's beautiful design for intimacy between a man and wife for a cheap simulation—pornography. We trade real community and real relationship for a miserable simulation—social media.

Nearly every story in this book thus far involved significant periods of waiting—at least decades, if not centuries. I've made the argument that God chooses to work over time to accomplish His will in our lives. Some of these stories have what you might call a happy ending or a good outcome, but most of them are not "happy" stories.

Do you think my dad was happy waking up in a hospital room with no arm at 16?

Do you think Oswald and Biddy were happy when he died at a young age with so much unfulfilled promise?

Do you think William Borden was happy when he faced death in Cairo having never reached the mission field to which he was called?

Do you think Pere Renou was happy toiling away in the Yunnan province without winning a single believer to Christ?

Do you think David Livingstone was happy fighting all manner of disease in Africa and eventually dying there, leaving behind only one convert?

I'm certain there were happy times in each of their lives, but I doubt seriously that happiness characterized their lives. But I also believe that what each of these people lacked in happiness, they made up for in joy. The Apostle Paul (a great long view story in its own right) said it this way in Colossians 1:24: "Now **I rejoice** in what I am suffering for you" (NIV, emphasis mine). What? Rejoice in suffering? Apparently so. Same author, different New Testament book: "But that's not all! We **gladly suffer**, because we know that suffering helps us to endure. And endurance builds character, which gives us a hope that will never disappoint us. All of this happens because God has given us the Holy Spirit, who fills our hearts with his love" (Rom. 5:3–5 CEV, emphasis mine).

> *"He's not concerned with your happiness. He's concerned with bigger things, deeper things."*

The church has been fed a distorted truth. I've had people sit in my office and justify all kinds of horrible behavior with the tilted logic of "God wants me to be happy." That falsehood has been used to justify adultery, divorce, abuse, bad financial decisions, and much more. It's a fake theology that allows us to use *our version* of God to justify doing whatever we want. But it's a lie. God doesn't want you to be happy, and He doesn't want you to be miserable either. God is indifferent to the momentary, fleeting feeling you capture in your eight seconds. He's not concerned with your happiness. He's concerned with bigger things, deeper things. Is your life on a trajectory toward Christlikeness? Is your life bringing Him glory? Do you have a deep-seated joy unwrinkled by circumstances?

There is joy available for you in the waiting room. The God of the long view doesn't make you wait for no reason. Go deeper. Lean into Him. Don't settle for the pursuit of something that is merely a simulation. You were made for more. He promised: "When you cross deep rivers, I will be with you, and you won't drown. When you walk through fire, you won't be burned or scorched by the flames" (Isa 43:2 CEV).

How do you find joy while you wait or even while you suffer? First Peter 4 helps us understand. I want to highlight several keys to finding joy while you wait, while you suffer, or maybe just while you live day to day:

1. Don't be surprised when things don't go your way (1 Peter 4:12).

Don't be surprised when you suffer or when you wait. It's part of God's plan. This isn't a mistake. God isn't confused. This moment isn't meaningless. This suffering, this waiting is a part of God's plan for your life—His will.

2. God isn't mad at you and He hasn't left you.

We are tested in the waiting room not because God is mad at us or hates us, but because He loves us so much He will go to any length necessary to restore us to Himself—even suffering. Suffering isn't a surprise. Waiting isn't an accident. They have a purpose. God is still right where He has always been. He hasn't left you.

3. Remember you aren't alone (1 Peter 4:13).

When we suffer, we suffer *with* Christ. I remember hearing that teaching as a child: Suffering is good because it identifies us with Christ and what He went through on the cross. When we suffer, we do identify with Christ. That teaching is right, but it's also incomplete. We suffer with Him, but He also suffers with us.

Here's a paradox of suffering: We don't overcome by overcoming. The methods of the world are overcoming, defeating, and killing. The overcoming methods of the Kingdom are suffering, self-sacrifice, and dying. The world wins by killing. Jesus wins by dying. Because Jesus suffers and dies *with* us, we are born again into something beautiful.

"Jesus lost all his glory so that we could be clothed in it. He was shut out so we could get access. He was bound, nailed, so that we could be free. He was cast out so we could approach. And Jesus took away the only kind of suffering that can really destroy you: that is being cast away from God. He took that so that now all suffering that comes into your life will only make you great. A lump of coal under pressure becomes a diamond. And the suffering of a person in Christ only turns you into somebody gorgeous."[25]

> **"The world wins by killing. Jesus wins by dying."**

4. Your suffering now is connected to God's eternal glory (1 Peter 4:13, 16).

We have joy in suffering here so we can have the fullness of His joy in eternity. Joy is available in the waiting room. You can have peace knowing that the God of the long view is at work in you. And ultimately, it will all work out for your good and His glory.

---

[25] Timothy Keller. *Walking with God Through Pain and Suffering*. New York: Penguin Books, 2013. 180–181.

It's all for God's glory. The answered prayers, yes. The miracles, yes. The salvation of thousands, yes. But the unanswered prayers, also yes. The delay or waiting, also yes. Those who hear and don't respond, also yes. Even the suffering, yes. The God of the long view will work it all out for your good and His glory. Just be patient. Just wait.

I don't think Tom Bodett was actually that far off. Remember he said, "A person needs just three things to be truly happy in this world: someone to love, something to do, and something to hope for." He was close, but he settled for a simulation when he could have offered the real thing. Here's my take: To have joy in the waiting room and in this world and beyond, a Christian really only needs three things—someone to love (Jesus), something to do (give God glory and follow His commands), and something to hope for (eternity with God).

> Beware of the temptation of leaning upon your understanding, with its clear strong thoughts. They only help you know what the heart must get from God—in themselves they are only images and shadows... Cultivate the greatest confidence that though you cannot see into your heart, God is working there by the Holy Spirit. Let the heart wait at times in perfect silence and quiet: in its hidden depths God will work. Be sure of this, and just wait on Him.[26]

---

[26] Andrew Murray. *Waiting on God*. Scotts Valley, CA: CreateSpace Independent Publishing Platform, 2017. 23.

My dad wasn't necessarily happy every step of the way, but he certainly found joy in the waiting room. So did Dr. Livingstone, Oswald Chambers, Pere Renou, and the rest.

CHAPTER 14

~~WE WIN~~
WE FINISH

"I don't understand Your ways
Oh but I will give You my song
Give You all of my praise
You hold on to all my pain
With it You are pulling me closer
And pulling me into Your ways
Now around every corner
And up every mountain
I'm not looking for crowns
Or the water from fountains
I'm desperate in seeking, frantic believing
That the sight of Your face
Is all that I need
I will say to You
It's gonna be worth it
It's gonna be worth it
It's gonna be worth it all
I believe this..."

RITA SPRINGER

My boys, Nathan and Adam, both grew up in the "we don't keep score" era of little league baseball. I remember thinking the whole thing was kind of silly, but everyone else seemed to think it was better for my kids if we didn't keep score. One day after one of Adam's very early tee ball games, we got in the car to go for ice cream. I congratulated him on a great game and relived a couple of parent highlights. Then he asked the question I wasn't ready for:

"Dad, did I win?"

"Well, son, you see, we weren't keeping score because at this point in your development as a player and athlete, it's best you focus on skill development and teamwork" (I was really proud of this answer. I had been properly indoctrinated by the little league "no keeping score" apostles). I assumed my brilliant parenting and eloquent answer would be satisfactory. But it wasn't.

"But dad, we had six runs and the other team only had three. That means we won, right?"

"Yes, Adam. It means your team won."

A full fist pump from the backseat was followed by an exuberant yell: "YES! I LOVE WINNING!"

And don't we all? We love winning. So even in places where we know we aren't supposed to keep score, we do. Church attendance? Converts? Baptisms? Someone in the church always keeps a tally.

I preach, but my dad is a preacher. There's a distinction here that some may not appreciate. When I say my dad is a preacher, I mean that as the highest compliment. He's what you picture when you think "preacher." Suit and tie (dad mowed the lawn in dress pants because he never owned a pair of jeans). The 10-pound Bible. The hankie in the air. The voice. The kind of preacher that starts slowly and somewhat softly and builds to a crescendo. Some preachers circle the airport and never land the plane, they never get to the point. But my dad landed the plane, he got to the point, straight down the runway, every single time.

I remember when I was a boy hearing my dad preach about God and His plan for humanity many times. I remember him talking about the task of reaching the lost. I remember him opining about the increasing secularization of our world and the church. He would paint a pretty powerful, if not desperate, picture of the world we live in, and then he would pick up his 10-pound Bible, wave it around, and say, "But don't be discouraged, friend. I've read this book from

Genesis to maps [a line that might be lost on a generation that now reads the Bible via an app]. I've read the last book. I've read the last chapter. I've read the last verse. And I have good news! I'm gonna get out of this thing alive even if it kills me! WE WIN!"

I don't preach (or write) with the same old-school fervor that my dad did, but I do believe this: God will be faithful to complete the long restoration He began in Genesis 3. We have this confident hope that God is faithfully chasing after His creation. The Creator will be reconciled with His creation. God's commissions will be fulfilled, and God will be glorified along every longitude and latitude. God's name will be made great among every nation, every tribe, every tongue, and every people.

There are moments in all of our stories in which it doesn't look like we will win, but nevertheless, win we will. If we can stretch our patience, our attention span, and our perspective to see the remainder of what is God is doing behind the scenes and through the ages, we will have the same confidence as my dad. We win!

WE'RE GOING TO FINISH!

June 6, 1994 was the 50th anniversary of the Allied invasion of Normandy, which began the historic World War II battle to liberate continental Europe from Nazi control. All the major television networks ran anniversary programs that included interviews with aging veterans. One program paired two contrasting interviews back to back. The first interview was with a marine who landed on

Omaha Beach. He recalled horrors that sounded like scenes from Steven Spielberg's Academy Award-winning movie *Saving Private Ryan*. The aging veteran recalled looking at the bloody casualties surrounding him and concluding, "We're going to lose!" The next interview featured a U. S. Army Air Corps reconnaissance pilot who flew over the whole battle area. He viewed the carnage on the beaches and hills, but he also witnessed the successes of the marines, the penetration of the paratroopers, and the effectiveness of the aerial bombardment. He looked at everything that was happening below and concluded, "We're going to win!"

We're simply living a line on a page. We just lived through A, B, and C, and we can barely imagine surviving to reach D. But the God who drew the line on the page also created the page on which the line was drawn, and He sees you passing D all the way to the end. The God of the long view has not given up on you and He won't. From His perspective, He can see all the ground His Kingdom gains, and God knows, He will accomplish His purposes in and through us.

I'm not nearing the end of my life (hopefully), but I am reaching the end of this book, and I'm reflecting on the values we place on accomplishment and placement. Paul also reflected on those values at the end of his life when he wrote to Timothy.

> Now the time has come for me to die. My life is like a drink offering being poured out on the altar. I have fought well. I have finished the race, and I have been faithful. So a crown

will be given to me for pleasing the Lord. He judges fairly, and on the day of judgment he will give a crown to me and to everyone else who wants him to appear with power. (2 Timothy 4:6–8 CEV)

We place value on winning in the West. In the words of the great philosopher Ricky Bobby, "If you ain't first, you're last!" And that's pretty true today in our culture. We care about the person who wins. Unless it was your team, it's unlikely you can tell me which team lost in any national championship game of any sport in the last decade—because it doesn't really matter to us. Winning matters more.

But Kingdom values are different. The Kingdom of God values finishing over winning. Paul doesn't indicate if he was first or second or second-to-last in the race, he just says, "I have finished the race" (2 Tim. 4:7). Finishing is what matters in the Kingdom. We imagine life as this great race to the finish line. We chase, we race, and we desperately

> *"We chase, we race, and we desperately want to finish first, but God sees everyone crossing at the same time. What matters to the God of the long view is that you finish."*

want to finish first, but God sees everyone crossing at the same time. What matters to the God of the long view is that you *finish*.

My encouragement to you is this—don't stop until you cross the finish line. Finish the race. Don't give up on the God of the long view because He certainly hasn't given up on you. He will patiently see you through to the end. When you do cross the finish line, you will look around and see Pere Renou, Dr. David Livingstone, and John Mark the evangelist. You will walk shoulder to shoulder in eternity with men and women who went before you and remained faithful to the God of the long view.

In eternity, we will connect the dots that are not clear here. We will step back and see that God had a plan all along. Things we saw as random were a part of His plan. He wasn't stuck in traffic or thrown for a loop by our circumstances—all of it was on purpose and for a purpose. In eternity, we will see that God was chasing after us the whole time.

What a shame if we worked our fingers to the bone trying to put up a winning time in a race with no race clock in sight! What if we tried so hard to win that we never finished? I'm not saying we shouldn't try; I'm saying we should put our efforts toward different things. Rather than working to impress with the biggest crowd or the greatest "success" story, let's put all our energy into knowing Him and making Him known. Let's push our missionaries, our pastors, and our churches to finish strong. Let's glorify God and do what

He commands, and let's acknowledge that it might look different in Dallas than it does in Djibouti, it might look different in Atlanta than it does in Azerbaijan. Let's remember that God isn't keeping score, and neither should we. He's just cheering for all of His kids to cross the finish line.

While it's not nearly as catchy or tweetable, maybe we need to change our mantra from "We win!" to "I've read the last page and *we finish!*"

Stacey King played for the Chicago Bulls, and one night after a great win, a reporter asked him what he would remember about this game. King responded, "I'll always remember this as the night that Michael Jordan and I combined to score 70 points." Jordan had scored a career high 69 points that night and Stacey King made one free throw...for one lousy point. But King and Jordan still won the game.

Yes, Jesus is triumphant. Jesus *wins*. And because Jesus wins, we win. But we need to remember that we aren't called to be the leading scorer—we are called to finish. Trying to be the leading scorer on a team with Jesus is like Stacey King trying to be the star of the game when he played with Michael Jordan. Let Jesus be Jesus, and you will win; try to be the star of the game and you'll lose your sanity and maybe a whole lot more.

Some of you say that you follow me, and others claim to follow Apollos. Isn't that how ordinary people behave? Apollos and I are merely servants who helped you to have faith. It was the Lord who made it all happen. I planted the seeds, Apollos watered them, but God made them sprout and grow. What matters isn't those who planted or watered, but God who made the plants grow. The one who plants is just as important as the one who waters. And each one will be paid for what they do. Apollos and I work together for God, and you are God's garden and God's building. (1 Cor. 3:4–9 CEV)

Paul and Apollos were a part of the New Testament "No Keeping Score" League. We should join them and focus on finishing.

CHAPTER 15

KEEP PLANTING

*"Don't judge each day by the harvest you reap
but by the seeds you plant."*

ROBERT LOUIS STEVENSON

In the summer of 2016, I visited Tunis, the capital of Tunisia, to examine the possibility of growing the church in this very difficult place. When I arrived and checked into my hotel room, there was a small gift bag on the desk. This was not an unusual occurrence for me, but at least one of the items in the gift bag stood out. Usually, a welcome gift contained a bottle of water, snacks for the room, a map of the local area, breath mints, etc. This welcome bag had a lot of those amenities, but along with them was a rather unusual welcome gift: a bottle of olive oil.

I asked our host at dinner that night about the unique gift, and he proceeded to educate me on the olive oil industry in Tunisia. I learned that Tunisia is the fourth largest producer of olive oil in the world behind three larger countries: Spain, Italy, and Greece. Olive oil is a big deal in Tunisia and a source of national pride. Today, olive oil is a major industry there, but it wasn't always so.

I often wonder how trends and industries develop in places like this, and a friend on the trip gave me a clue as to how the industry began. He shared a Latin inscription found on a tombstone in Uppena just down the coast from modern day Tunis. The inscription is over 1,500 years old (from the first half of the 5th century). The Latin inscription reads: *P(ius) v(ir) Dion bixsit annos octogenta et instituit arbores quatuor milia.*[27] Translated to English, this inscription says, "Here lies Dion, a pious man; he lived 80 years and planted 4,000 (olive) trees." The life of Dion doesn't appear in any chronicles anywhere else. Apparently, he was not remarkable in a historic sense: He didn't conquer empires or rule a nation. He was just an ordinary guy. He lived. He planted trees. He died. That's it.

But it seems Dion understood the long view. An olive tree may take more than a decade to start producing olives. We don't know if Dion lived long enough to see all of his olive trees, or any of his trees, start to produce fruit. But apparently that wasn't the point for Dion. His inscription doesn't say, "Here lies Dion. He lived 80 years and made a fortune in the olive industry." He simply planted. But today, because of unknown people like Dion, there is an olive industry large enough to impact the world commodities market. An olive tree can live over 2,000 years. Many of the olive trees Dion planted are likely alive today and produce olives that contribute to a major export for Tunisia.

Dion planted so someone else could harvest. Dion was what Cardinal Dearden called a "prophet of a future not his own." And so are we.

---

[27] *Inscriptiones latines de la Tunisie (ILT)*, 243.

Would it be enough for you if what you planted today didn't produce fruit in your lifetime? It was enough for Dion. And for Pere Renou. It was enough for Apollos and Paul. And it should be for you and me.

PLANTING A SEED

I remember a sermon my dad preached at a funeral when I was young. He talked about the "dash between the dates." We're all born. We all die. It's what we do with the dash between the dates that matters. What if my "dash" is all planting and no reaping? What if my "dash" is all toiling and no winning? What if my "dash" is composed of prayers that someone else is the answer to centuries from now? What if my "dash" is all for things not seen and victories not won yet for generations? What if other people are bringing in truckloads of olives while I'm still planting seeds that are yet to become trees? Can I learn to be okay with all of that and to rejoice in it?

> *"We're all born. We all die. It's what we do with the dash between the dates that matters."*

I'm not there yet, but I am learning to be a seed planter and trusting God to do the rest. The morning I wrote this chapter, I planted a seed. I didn't do it because I was writing a book, and it didn't occur to me at the time that I was even "planting," but I think I was.

It was a Saturday morning, three days before Christmas. I left the house and headed to the office to write. I stopped at my local gas station, as I do every morning, for a 54-ounce unsweet iced tea. Three patrons in front of me in line was a young boy (perhaps 6-years-old) buying a bag of M&M's. He was paying with all pennies and few nickels. Normally, this kind of behavior annoys me, but something about the boy stood out to me. He had just enough money to buy the M&M's and gave a little fist pump as he walked away from the register. I watched as he left the convenience store and climbed into the backseat of a GMC pickup that was at least 30 years old—not vintage and cool, just old and rundown.

The line was moving particularly slowly, so I watched as the little boy wrestled with the bag of M&M's and then passed them around to share with his little sister next to him and his dad in the front seat. I wondered if this was their breakfast, and I felt like the Lord told me to help them. I had a $100 bill in my pocket designated for my iced tea and a last-minute Christmas gift I was picking up on my way to the office.

I stepped out of line, sat my tea on the counter, and walked out to the truck. As I approached the truck, the dad slowly cranked the window down about halfway (it occurred to me in this moment that I must not look very dangerous). I reached in my pocket, grabbed the $100 bill, and handed it to him. Defensively, he snapped, "What's this for?" I opened my mouth and these words came out: "Jesus told me to give this to you, so you could do something nice for your kids for Christmas." I turned to walk back into the store and as I did, he grabbed my arm. He was shaking. "Did Jesus say anything else?" he asked. I opened my mouth and again these words just came out: "He said to tell you He hasn't forgotten you." I turned to walk away again, and I heard him say confidently, "The Lord sure is mysterious."

I walked back into the store and finished paying for my iced tea (with my debit card) and began to carry on with my day. I didn't feel particularly good about the exchange. Don't get me wrong, I was content that I had been obedient. But I replayed the exchange in my mind and wondered what I might have said differently or "better." I don't know how you are, but when I self-analyze situations like this, good, confident thoughts enter my head slowly while bad, insecure thoughts rush in violently and in legions: "I should have invited them to church. I should have told him not to spend it on cigarettes. I should have prayed with him. I should have offered to go shopping with them to make sure he spent 'my' money wisely. I should have said different things. I should have learned his name." I paid for my tea and looked outside again. The dad was obviously crying. He wiped the tears from his face the way one man does when he realizes another man has "caught" him crying. Then he looked at me and smiled. As I got in my truck to pull out of the parking lot, I could see him behind me, still wiping tears from his face.

RELEASING A SEED

All the way to the office, I kicked myself for not doing better. I sat down to pick up with my writing. The next ideation on my story board was "planting seeds." I wrote half of the chapter before I realized that the regret I felt over planting the seed and not harvesting anything that morning was a lesson for me—and maybe now for you, too.

God designed us to plant. I mean, think about your hand for a minute. You can hold a seed (an actual seed, $100 bill, or something else) in your hand, but you can't *plant* that seed until you open your hand and turn it loose. How many seeds could you plant? Thousands? Maybe millions? An unimaginable number of seeds could pass through your hands in a lifetime. As long as you are willing to let a seed go, your hand is designed for the work of planting. How much harvest are able to hold onto? Only a handful until you must entrust the harvest to some other storage method. We can clinch the harvest tightly, but as long as we do, we will not be able to use our hands to plant another seed.

> *"If we become obsessed with the outcome of the seeds we plant, we will certainly plant fewer seeds."*

This is our choice: We can hold tightly to a handful of harvest or we can have open hands and allow the Lord of the harvest to provide both the seed and the harvest. If we become obsessed with the outcome of the seeds we plant, we will certainly plant fewer seeds. But if we plant seeds and trust God to send someone else to water them, we can continue to plant and nurture seeds, knowing that ultimately God will cause the growth of all the seeds and bring about the harvest.

Dion in Tunisia kept on planting. If he had planted a seed and then waited 10 or 12 years until the tree produced olives before he planted another seed, he might have planted six or seven trees in his lifetime. But instead he planted 4,000. Why? Because he trusted the life in the seed and he believed that over time rain would fall, the sun would shine, and eventually the seed would grow into a tree and produce olives. Dion understood that the part he could control was planting the seed. He understood the long view. So, he planted, and so should we.

I will make this personal and make no accusation or assumption about where you are. I, for one, need to learn to be less obsessed with outcomes and to find satisfaction in the process of planting and nurturing. I need to become more comfortable with unfinished stories. I need to remember that I'm not writing the stories anyway. I'm just part of God's global plan for restoring His creation to Himself. I will keep planting seeds whether I see the harvest or not. I will keep planting seeds even if someone else harvests and gets the credit for it (remember, we're not keeping score). I will thank God that I'm part of His master plan. I'll rejoice that I am a minister, not a messiah. I will trust that the God of the long view has a plan, knows the plan, and is working out His plan in me even when I can't see the seed growing or producing. I will live. I will die. And with the dash between my birth and death, I will keep planting seeds and trust there is life in those seeds whether I live to see them grow or not.

EPILOGUE

*"Such a large crowd of witnesses is all around us! So we must get rid of
everything that slows us down, especially the sin that just won't let go. And
we must be determined to run the race that is ahead of us. We must keep
our eyes on Jesus, who leads us and makes our faith complete. He endured
the shame of being nailed to a cross, because he knew that later on he
would be glad he did. Now he is seated at the right side of God's throne! So
keep your mind on Jesus, who put up with many insults from sinners.
Then you won't get discouraged and give up.*

*None of you have yet been hurt in your battle against sin. But you have
forgotten that the Scriptures say to God's children,*

> *'When the Lord punishes you,*
> *don't make light of it,*
> *and when he corrects you,*
> *don't be discouraged.*
> *The Lord corrects the people*
> *he loves*
> *and disciplines those*
> *he calls his own.'*

*Be patient when you are being corrected! This is how God treats his
children. Don't all parents correct their children? God corrects all of his
children, and if he doesn't correct you, then you don't really belong to*

him. Our earthly fathers correct us, and we still respect them. Isn't it even better to be given true life by letting our spiritual Father correct us?

Our human fathers correct us for a short time, and they do it as they think best. But God corrects us for our own good, because he wants us to be holy, as he is. It is never fun to be corrected. In fact, at the time it is always painful. But if we learn to obey by being corrected, we will do right and live at peace.

Now stand up straight! Stop your knees from shaking and walk a straight path. Then lame people will be healed, instead of getting worse."

HEBREWS 12:1–14 (CEV)

There's a Chinese Proverb that says, "A journey of a thousand miles begins with a single step."

It's hard to argue with that logic. The point of the proverb is clear: You'll never get to the end of a journey if you don't start with the first step. Again, nothing wrong with that.

Perhaps the point of this book is to remind you that a journey of a thousand miles ends with step number 1,857,992 (if anyone wants to actually walk a thousand miles and dispute this calculated number, I'll gladly edit it in future editions).

In that journey of a thousand miles, you will make some wrong turns. In that journey of a thousand miles, you will take some detours and distractions.

In that journey of a thousand miles, you will step in some mud puddles, or worse.

In that journey of a thousand miles, you will wear out your shoes... several times.

You will have to stop for rest. You will need help. You will get discouraged.

Most of us are somewhere in the middle of the journey, and most of us need reminding that the journey is worth it. The journey from step number one to step number 1,857,992 is all part of the God of the long view's plan for you. It's not random or reckless. It's beautifully mapped out by Him.

> If you do what the Lord wants,
>> he will make certain
>> each step you take is sure.
> The Lord will hold your hand,
>> and if you stumble,
>> you still won't fall. (Psalm 37:23–24 CEV)

Use every step to glorify God. Every victory, every failure, every win, every loss, every right step, and every wrong one can bring Him glory.

Try not to be afraid of heights. Every now and then, climb to a high place and take a look back on where you've been. Focus your eyes and watch the dots connect on the page. Get a glimpse of what God is up to. And then...go finish.

When God acts miraculously and a 1,000-year work is accomplished in a day, bring Him glory. When God acts over time and a day-long work is accomplished in 1,000 years, bring Him glory.

Finish strong. Bring Him glory.

It helps, now and then, to step back and take a long view.

The Kingdom is not only beyond our efforts, it is even beyond our vision.

We accomplish in our lifetime only a tiny fraction of the magnificent enterprise that is God's work. Nothing we do is complete, which is a way of saying that the Kingdom always lies beyond us.

No statement says all that could be said.

No prayer fully expresses our faith.

No confession brings perfection.

No pastoral visit brings wholeness.

No program accomplishes the Church's mission.

No set of goals and objectives includes everything.

This is what we are about.

We plant the seeds that one day will grow.

We water seeds already planted, knowing that they hold future promise.

We lay foundations that will need further development.
We provide yeast that produces far beyond our capabilities.

We cannot do everything, and there is a sense of liberation in realizing that.

This enables us to do something, and to do it very well.

It may be incomplete, but it is a beginning, a step along the way, an opportunity for the Lord's grace to enter and do the rest.

We may never see the end results, but that is the difference between the master builder and the worker.

We are workers, not master builders; ministers, not messiahs.

We are prophets of a future not our own.

CARDINAL DEARDEN

ABOUT THE AUTHOR

David Wigington grew up in a pastor's home and preached his first sermon when he was 11-years-old. He is passionate about communications, missions, and church planting and has a heart for the lost. He travels around the world to engage, encourage, and equip missionary workers and pastors in over 50 countries. He and his wife Shana pioneered Cornerstone Christian Fellowship in Bloomington, Indiana in 1997. Cornerstone is consistently among the top 25 missions giving churches in the Assemblies of God. David serves on the board of The Stone Table and the elder board of Live Dead. He has helped raise over $30 million for missions in his lifetime. David and Shana have two sons, Nathan and Adam, and will soon add two daughters-in-love, Brianna and Rachel, to their family. David enjoys golf, photography, and reading.